DATE DUE

Nobody Said It's Easy

Nobody Said It's Easy

A PRACTICAL GUIDE TO FEELINGS AND RELATIONSHIPS FOR YOUNG PEOPLE AND THEIR PARENTS

Sally Liberman Smith

ILLUSTRATED BY ROY DOTY

The Macmillan Company, New York
Collier-Macmillan Limited, London

Copyright © Sally Liberman Smith 1965

All rights reserved. No part of this book may be reproduced or utilized in any form or by any means, electronic or mechanical, including photo-copying, recording or by any information storage and retrieval system, without permission in writing from the publisher.

First Printing

The Macmillan Company, New York
Collier-Macmillan Canada Ltd., Toronto, Ontario

Library of Congress catalog card number: 64–19992

Printed in the United States of America

Dedicated to

my favorite explorers

who don't dig easy answers,

Bob,

Randy, Nicky, Gary,

and Mom and Dad

ACKNOWLEDGMENTS

To my family, which has helped me widen my inner lenses, my thanks and my love.

To Mrs. Liebe Kravitz I am indebted for her friendship and interest, her complete frankness, astute criticism, and profound advice.

To Mary Lystad, Maureen Nelson, Joan Blos, Edna Salant, Claire Bloomberg, my grateful thanks for critical reading of the manuscript in progress and helpful suggestions.

To Uncle Paul Elkin, my fondest appreciation for editorial critiques.

My warmest thanks to Irving Salomon, whose invitations to Rancho Lilac gave our family the relaxation that gave me the energy to write a book.

My appreciation to Kiriki for all that she has gone through with me on this work.

To Mary and Lawrence K. Frank, to Dr. Nina Ridenour, to my college and graduate-school professors Smitty, Dr. Ned Hall, Dr. Erich Fromm, Dr. Arnold Rose, and Dr. Howard Lane, who helped guide me to the threshold of my own mind, my gratitude. I have not forgotten nor will I forget the inspiration and guidance they all have given me, plus their encouragement to keep learning, questioning, thinking.

Contents

Preface

This book was completed before that agonizing date in American history, November 22, 1963. I feel I cannot leave unwritten a few words concerning President Kennedy's assassination, particularly in a book for young people exploring feelings and relationships.

President Kennedy was a leader of this age who ignited the fire of young people. He himself was young, courageous, modern. He symbolized a trust in youth, a burning faith in the future. Suddenly he was taken away from us by tyranny—the tyranny of inner forces that can destroy people and even nations. Fear, frustration, guilt, hate, a sense of failure, a sense of defeat and worthlessness—these were some of the inner forces that burst forth to destroy our young President.

Strong feelings, pushed underground, stored away in the recesses of the mind, can control the way we live our lives. Reason and responsibility are kindled by knowledge of these forces inside ourselves. Our survival depends upon our ability to employ reason, and today every single one of us needs to assume more responsibility than has ever before burdened human beings.

*

Nobody Said It's Easy is a book designed to launch individual exploration inside and around ourselves. It is easier to look outward at other people than to look inward. It is never easy to gain and to maintain an inside track on ourselves—on our own feelings and relationships.

The preparation for launching exploration of outer space today is rough, rigorous, demanding, carefully planned, studied seriously and in depth, evaluated, re-evaluated, re-re-evaluated, constantly changing to meet new needs. But what preparation do we have for exploring our feelings, our relationships?

We study, we plan, we prepare for almost everything in life except our relationships. And what do we spend our whole lives doing except relating to other human beings! We relate to our relations, our teachers, our friends, our enemies; we relate to persons of the opposite sex, to employers, to officials, to strangers, to older people, to younger people; we relate eventually to our mates, our children, our in-laws, our grandchildren, and to countless others every single day of our lives. Yet, do we stop and take a good look at how we get along with others?

Some of us think about our relationships. Most of us don't. Other's won't. *Why?* Some of us plunge into and out of relationships with abandon, and our lives are influenced by the rise and fall of these relationships.

There are no foolproof formulas, no preplanned destinations, no predictable returns for establishing and maintaining relationships. *Nobody Said It's Easy* (and it isn't!) explores some of the limitless frontiers needing to be crossed by each of us, every day, in our own unique ways. There are some tracking stations, some signals, some forms of equipment that we can develop, and these human tools we shall pursue in this book.

Nobody Said It's Easy

Our parents have more to do with the design of our lives than we like to admit.

1. Relations

It is out of relations that we come to be. We all have
relations of one sort or another—family relations, social
relations, community relations, international relations. Our
present and future relations are greatly determined by our
past relations. ③

Ordinarily, parents are our first and most influential
relations. Ordinarily, it is first with our parents that we establish paths of getting along with others, paths of communication and affection. ②

Relations is a meaningful word, for in itself it implies
that the ways in which we relate to others have to do with
the ways in which we relate to our parents. Our parents
have more to do with the design of our lives than we like
to admit. Even parents fail to realize how much control
they have over us and how much of our own piloting
through life is directed by them. The vast area of our
personal relations can be as unprobed as outer space—
and even more so. Let's begin by probing parents.

Our parents were children once. They had parents who
loved them a lot, loved them some, or loved them not so
much.

Their parents trained, taught, disciplined them

Their parents made many demands upon them

Their parents may have had high expectations for them

Their parents were subject to economic, social, business, community, emotional pressures

Their parents were at times confused, inconsistent, unreasonable, irritable

Their parents did or did not have faith in them

Their parents were often at odds with our parents, particularly when our parents were teenagers struggling to develop their own unique personalities and to become independent

Although some of us wonder about our parents' intentions, it is difficult to believe that there is a parent who purposely starts out to maltreat, punish, threaten, terrorize, or make miserable her child. The original intentions are usually good, but the actions of a parent can go contrary to the good intentions. Most parents try to do the very best they can for their children in so far as they are able and in so far as they know what the best is. A parent's "best" is culled from his experiences, his feelings, his relationships, his values, his goals, his way of life. Some people's "best" is better than others.

Sometimes parents don't realize that they do not like or respect themselves. If they do not respect and approve of themselves, they can hardly respect and approve of their children. If they are not satisfied with themselves, can parents be satisfied with their children?

The degree to which our parents were allowed by their parents to grow, to flourish, to develop themselves in large part determines the degree to which our parents can allow us to grow, to flourish, to develop ourselves, which may in turn influence the degree of freedom we shall allow our children.

Our parents often resemble their parents in personality, willingly or not, for better or for worse. Some parents tried to be just the opposite of their parents, and this can be disastrous too. Others are merely modified versions of their parents, having made some effort to change in themselves what they did not like in their parents. There are lots of good, loving parents in this world, although it is impossible for human beings who are parents to be "good" parents every bit of the time. And should they be? How could we ever learn to live with the imperfections in life if there were perfect parents and perfect children?

There are great satisfactions and thrills in parenthood, along with a lot of routine and distasteful tasks. Is it fun for parents to have to remind us to hurry for school, to wash our hands, to pick up, to stand up—when they know we don't want to—in order to shake hands with someone they could not care less about? When we are parents, we too shall find ourselves with distasteful tasks and responsibilities that we don't always like; we too shall be cross with exhaustion at times or impatient under the strain of so much responsibility. We may hear ourselves saying just what our parents said and may act with our children the way our parents acted with us. Hopefully, we shall have enough insight into the ways and means of parents and ourselves that we won't make the same mistakes our parents made. We shall make different ones, perhaps.

How our parents feel about us naturally influences how we feel about them. How we relate to our parents and to our brothers and sisters affects all our relationships. "Nonsense," you might think. But remember that sarcastic tone of voice your father used to tease you? Now think about the teacher, the employer, the neighborhood boy who may have used the same tone of voice. Didn't you react to him in almost the same way as you did to your father? As for your mother's sense of martyrdom—accompanied by a certain expression on her face and that oh-so-familiar tone of voice—don't you react to anyone else like that whom you come within a hairbreadth of in somewhat the same way as you do to your mother? Someone who is on the defensive most of the time at home is likely to be keeping score in almost all his relationships. For the girl whose relationship with her parents is one of avoiding real contact with them as much as possible, doesn't that wall separate her from other people?

The successful ways we have found to obtain approval from our parents, we translate into all our relationships. We may not even realize it. Unconsciously, we know what our parents like, want, and need. The bookworm who spews out facts to all who will listen is likely to have received approval from her parents for all her knowledge, so this is how she tries to please others. Hard work and self-sacrifice get approval in some families to the exclusion of everything else, so some children feel they can please others only by working hard and being self-sacrificing. What about the boy whose parents are interested only in his virility and athletic prowess—isn't he likely to be busy showing off the hair on his chest? Or might he do just the opposite?

Sometimes we do just the reverse of what our parents want and like. This too gets translated into our relationships. Often parents who overstress neatness have children who assert themselves through their messiness. If we stop and think about what our parents like most about us, we may be surprised to see how we, without thinking about it, play up or play down these qualities in other relationships. Even the parents who genuinely love us and accept us for what we are approve of certain of our qualities more than others.

As tiny infants we were not aware of the existence of others. There are a few fully grown infants in adult clothing who have never grown aware of the existence of others. But, happily, most of us learned early that there were others in the world. We showed our awareness of them when we smiled at them as they leaned over our cribs. We displayed our love and our dependence when we put our little hands into their big hands and squeezed hard. We became selves because we were treated as selves. We had our own names, things done just for us, stories told just about us, and we were the only ones in the world just like us! As infants we were completely dependent upon our parents for everything. Slowly we became less so. The world outside our home enlarged. The milkman, the postman, the delivery man, the neighbors, friends of our parents, and other children entered our lives. There were the community, a score of relatives, then the school, the church, other activities, and other people. Our friends became more and more important. We needed our parents less. Some parents did not want to be needed less and hung on to us tight, for there are emotionally deprived parents just as there are emotionally deprived and handicapped children. Some parents were growing with us and were therefore able to be needed less. Often we thought we were more independent of our parents than we really were.

Now is the time when most of us are struggling to become independent of, yet get on comfortably with, our parents. There is always much we are unsure of, much we are struggling against, much we resent. Some of us are able to admit that there is yet much we do not know. To untie the parental knots and stand on our own two feet serenely facing the big, complicated world is one of life's most difficult tasks, shared by all people everywhere. It is not easy to get a line on ourselves.

Emancipation does not necessarily mean repudiation. It is not an equation whereby emancipation equals the rejection of our parents. Those who make the loudest noises about being independent of their parents may not, in fact, have cut the ties or they would not need to protest so much. We can be independent personalities in our own right and still live in the same house as our parents. We can be extremely dependent upon our parents emotionally while living six thousand miles away earning our own living! There are some people too fearful even to try to become independent of their parents. There are others who spend their lives unsuccessfully trying to declare their independence. Some people can write like Thomas Jefferson but cannot live their independence. Most of us struggle and experience some painful moments but in time achieve our inner independence and establish good relationships with our parents. Often it isn't until after we revolt against our parents that we come to understand and realize how human they are. Then we can relate to each of them as one imperfect human being to another.

Some of us, in our struggle to become our own independent selves, aim for a goal that we can never achieve— and how awful if we could! That aim is toward total independence. But the world is not constructed like that. We need other people for companionship and comfort, for approval and disapproval, as well as to have homes, to have schools, to work.

We talk an awful lot about becoming independent of our parents, but what do we mean by this? Many of us take it to mean a whole host of "we don'ts":

> We don't want to be treated like babies.
> We don't want to be told what to do.
> We don't want to be preached at.
> We don't want to be criticized.
> We don't want to be pressured.
> We don't want restrictions.
> We don't want . . .

You can finish the list.

Knowing what we don't want is a first step. Some people stop right there. But most of us move on to what we do want. We can learn something from the experience of citizens of the newly independent countries in Asia and Africa. Having rebelled against their rulers, they knew well what they did not want. They resented outside control, manipulation, exploitation, unnecessary restrictions, lack of respect, and lack of opportunity. To varying degrees, they knew what they wanted. They demanded and they won the freedom to be themselves, to control their own affairs, to decide what was best for them and what was not, to express their own opinions and feelings without fear, to be free to make their own mistakes, to feel entirely comfortable in their own territory. All this was not achieved immediately, some of it is still being achieved, and some is yet to be achieved. Countries, like people, have to work hard to maintain independence. Few of the newly independent countries were prepared for the amount of responsibility involved in freedom. Few were aware of the countless numbers of decisions that had to be made every day, how choices had to be made at every turn, how every choice meant the giving up of one thing for another.

Young people too want the freedom to be themselves. They want to control their own affairs, decide what is best for them, enrich themselves in certain areas and not in others, choose their own friends, and make their own commitments. On the basis of the experience and knowledge we have, we design our own standards, develop our own values, and, hopefully, learn from our own mistakes. We wish to think for ourselves, express our own opinions, and develop and act on our own convictions. Becoming independent of our parents is a process whereby we take all the matter they have given us, wanted and unwanted, and reassemble it in a unique form that constitutes what we are. Who are we?

Do you know that cozy feeling of being off by yourself somewhere, sort of talking to yourself, and suddenly being so elated by the thought "I'm *me*!" that you want to pinch yourself to see if it's true? Have you ever looked at your hand—its shape, its form, the way it opens and closes, how it grabs and straightens out, how it moves, the fascinating lines that run through it—have you looked at that hand and been aware that this is your hand, only yours, one of billions like it, yet very special and different? Stepping along on a cold windy day, have you ever stopped and thought about that tingling, sometimes exhilarating feeling inside that is tapping out a rhythm that is distinctly you? Standing on an empty subway platform or waiting for a bus on a dimly lit road, have you ever allowed yourself to feel that bleak sensation of complete aloneness?

Achieving independence is the process of separating out what is "us" from what is our parents. We can never totally isolate one from the other. There is always a connection, however remote. Separating out begins with opening up and examining the matter. We separate out our parents' interests, likes, dislikes, needs, values, standards, thought patterns, ways of acting as distinct from our own—or what we would like to be our own. The paths our parents have found for themselves may not suit us. What makes sense for us may not be suitable for them. To separate out is not to judge one as absolutely right and one as absolutely wrong. The separating out is more subtle. It is discovering what suits our unique personalities best. There may be some or many interests, likes, dislikes, values, ways of thinking and acting that our parents and we can share in common. Separating out our unique selves means determining as far as we can what our real feelings are. Without knowing it, we may be feeling what our parents want or don't want us to feel rather than what we might feel without parental influence. Our relations with others may be governed by feelings we do not recognize.

The extent to which life makes us or we make life is what counts. Some people feel that life just happens. If things just happen to them all through life, they feel they are not responsible for anything. Certainly we are not responsible for ourselves if life just happens to us and governs us. By separating out what is us and what is our parents, we come to know ourselves, our inner space, and we are no longer flying by wire.

Independence means gaining an infinite number of responsibilities. We are quite responsible for ourselves. Whereas our parents automatically said "no" before, and we accepted what they said or fought against what they said or wished we had fought against what they said, our independence means we must evaluate the situation for what it is worth. We make decisions for ourselves, taking our own lives into our own hands.

Just like the newly independent countries, we are busy making choices with our independence. Each choice may mean giving up something we like for something we like more or choosing something we don't like over something we like even less or choosing something we like rather than something we don't like. There may even be situations in which we choose something we don't like rather than something we do like. Growing involves losing something while gaining something else. Making choices means taking risks. Being human means we are imperfect, so we make many mistakes. Some of our choices are not in keeping with what is right for us. Other people can advise us, and people are always eager to give advice; but we are the ones who take the risks, for we alone make the choices. The decision-making process can make us feel quite alone. Yet this very aloneness often brings us closer to other people, to our parents, and to ourselves.

The separating out of ourselves as unique human beings does not happen all at once with a push-button ease and a burst of glory. It is a many-stage process. Freedom is an internal experience. We have to come to know it and feel it individually. Biologists, as well as psychologists, tell us that all human beings (whether they know it or not), one way or another, resist restraints upon their freedom to be themselves. Press hard on the sole of a baby's foot; he presses back. Open his hands; he closes them. We instinctively react against the imposition of outside force. We react against being molded, manipulated, restrained.

It is right that we rebel to a certain extent against our parents in order to discover ourselves. We can't separate out what is "us" otherwise. This does not mean that we have a license to defy them at will. There are many forms of rebellion, but what we are after is a questioning spirit to help us identify ourselves. Human beings are human beings not only by virtue of believing but also by virtue of challenging belief. We differ from the animal world by virtue of our brain power, our imagination, and our ability to reason. Religious leaders and philosophers tell us that our brains and our hearts are miraculous, that we have something very precious to develop.

As children we plied our parents with questions. *Why* are there families? *Why* do we breathe? *Why* do we have only two legs? *Why* does the sun come up and go down? *Why, why, why* comes out of the child just learning to talk, and it keeps coming out all through life. Sometimes we don't listen to our own "whys." Maybe we are afraid to.

When we question and sometimes test out our parents, we are discovering and exploring them, as well as ourselves. Discovery usually inspires growth. Growth *can* bring about change. Change means changing ourselves. It is difficult and sometimes impossible to try to change our parents. We are not likely to succeed at that, and it is just a way of avoiding the responsibility of changing ourselves. When we were youngsters we could kill off our parents in just one dream and transform them magically into the kind of parents we wanted. But in the real world we are the ones who change—and hope that they will respond. The closer we come to being independent of our parents, the more our parents seem to change, because our own perspective changes and we often view life differently. Mark Twain once remarked that when he was fourteen, he could not get over how ignorant his father was; but by the time he, Twain, was twenty-one, he was greatly impressed to see how much the old man had learned. Perhaps by the time he was nearing thirty, he had developed a profound respect for his father, giving more weight to his outstanding qualities than to his limitations.

The roots and the routes of our relationships are determined in large measure by our parents, the kind of people they are, what forces created them, how we react and relate to them. Probing our parents helps us understand the roots. The roots we cannot change, but the routes we can change.

2. Feelings

THE FINEST SIGNALS ever created are part of us—our feelings. They are coded into the way we act. Like all good signals, they mean a lot. Our task is to learn to recognize and read these signals.

We are full of signals. They bid us to take notice. They alert us to danger. They warn us. They protect us. They flash the "go ahead" and reassure us that everything is O.K.

Every single one of us is full of feelings. Every single one of us has experienced happy, pleasant feelings. We have all experienced frightened, guilty, angry feelings. Every single one of us has had feelings we cannot decipher. There is a potpourri of feelings underneath all our behavior.

Sometimes we think we are the only ones in the whole wide world to have experienced a certain feeling. This is a nice thought when the feelings are happy, cozy ones. It is quite a terrifying thought when the feelings are angry, guilty, fearful ones. Although alone at the time with those feelings, we are not alone in experiencing them. We have company all over the world, for there is a universal bond of feelings. What provokes the feelings and how we express them differs widely from person to person, country to coun-

25

try, continent to continent. A smile may not mean happiness, a hard stare may not connote disapproval, tears may not express sadness, banging a shoe may not mean anger.

Normally each person is born with a fully developed capacity for feeling. We can practically see a baby's feelings. We can see a baby who was frightened by a loud noise relax physically and emotionally when he is tenderly comforted and reassured. Neglect him or hurt him and listen to the screams of anger. The mind seems to have very little to do with the capacity to feel. Both the mentally retarded child and the child with a stellar I.Q. are nourished on feelings and grow up feeling their way through life.

Feelings are aroused by all that we have experienced. They are aroused by what we see, what we hear, what we touch or what touches us, what we smell, and what we taste. Feelings are aroused by what is happening, by the situation we are in, by what we are reminded of, by what we remember.

Do you remember how huge the world seemed to you when you were very little, how big that sink was, how high the light switch, how hard to reach the top bureau drawer, how everything and everyone around you were so much bigger than you? Can you recapture for an instant the feeling of exultation you had when you were on top of the jungle gym? Do you remember how you felt when someone you admired put an arm around your shoulder or gave you a hug? If your parents argued in front of you, did this arouse feelings in you? Do certain smells bring out special memories within you?

What were your feelings on the first day at school or the first time you were allowed to cross the street by yourself and ride the bus alone? Girls, do you remember the first time your menstrual period began? And, boys, do you recall having a dream that was sexually arousing? Do you remember some of the feelings that were yours then? Can you recall a time when you were outside the door of someone's house ringing the bell and standing there all by yourself, with not a soul in sight? Perhaps you can flash back to an experience you had when you were one of many at a baseball game or squeezing into a subway train or standing around at an accident. How well can you remember the feelings that went along with these experiences? The feelings and experiences are usually woven together into a memory. Sometimes we misremember or distort an incident because the feelings that accompanied the incident were so strong that they overshadowed the incident itself.

Has there been a time recently when, at a party or at school or while visiting someone, you were aware of feeling the same way you did when you were a little child? We often forget feelings we had when we were children. It is very difficult to remember many things that happened to us when we were little, but surely we can remember a few incidents to which we had strong reactions. The feelings we experienced as little children influence our adult lives, whether we know it or not and often whether we like it or not.

Although we seem to forget or brush away a lot of what we are feeling, we talk a lot about feelings in our daily conversations. If you place a magnifying glass on our daily conversations, you may find that we employ the word *feeling* all the time and often in extraordinary ways. Look at these examples and add more of your own:

> How are you feeling?
> I feel funny about this.
> We feel this is logical.

He feels this is important to read.
What are your feelings about investments?
Do you feel this is a wise choice?
How do you feel about your teacher?
The class felt the comparison was valid.
They felt he had sufficient proof.
Where did you feel the film dragged?
We felt the lecture was brilliant.
They felt the launching was a success.

Isn't it curious that the word *feeling* is used by us so indiscriminately? Can we talk about feelings when discussing logic, proof, validity, a launching? Why has the word *feeling* crept into so much of our conversation, when so few of us are aware of our own feelings and rarely mention how we really feel inside? Perhaps it magnifies a recognition that what we feel may even be more important than what we say or do.

Some of us are in touch with our built-in signals. Some of us are only sporadically in touch. Some of us turn off our signals. Why?

Often the feelings that make people uncomfortable, they try to push away. The feelings associated with inner anguish are the ones we try to avoid or perhaps deny completely.

There are reasons why we are uncomfortable with certain feelings. Our parents, our friends, society in general may not approve of these feelings. We may have concluded on the basis of early experiences that these feelings are bad, and our having them makes us feel that we are bad. Our parents want us to be accepted and liked and approved of by the people who are important to them. If we want the approval of our parents (and down deep we do) most of us learn how to behave in a manner that gains their ap-

We learn early in life to cover up how we really feel.

proval. Often this leads to conflict—we feel one way and are pulled another. We learn very early in life to cover up how we really feel about things and about people.

Up to a point, this is reasonable. We cannot go around clubbing all who annoy us, kissing every person who makes us feel good, and unnecessarily hurting people by saying every single thing we feel about them. Letting our feelings run rampant or denying the very existence of our feelings is what causes difficulties for us. To have a feeling, to recognize it, to feel O.K. about it is not the same as a license to inflict it upon others. It is like freedom, which is not a license to do whatever appeals to us without considering the other people with whom we share a world.

There is nothing wrong with having feelings, even the nastiest ones we can conjure up. We all have them. Like almost everything else in life, it is not what we have that counts so much as what we do with what we have and why we do it.

It is appropriate in certain situations to hide feelings that we know we have. But hiding these feelings does not mean denying their very existence. As much as we may want to, we are incapable of pressing some slick buttons and turning our feelings off entirely. Hidden feelings are just stored somewhere in the vast empire that is "us" and come out in other places at other times.

Our parents have taught us how to eat with a spoon and a fork, to wash, to dress, to use a toilet, and to get along with other people. We may not approve of how they taught us these things or what they taught us, but they did it, and how they did it was based on their own experiences and the kind of people they are. They taught us to cover up certain feelings, not only by their spoken words but by their own examples. Often they taught us not only to cover up our feelings but also to be ashamed of them. They may not even be aware of this. Sometimes our shame was so great that we buried the feelings, just as they had done and perhaps their parents before them.

Was there a time when you said, "I hate you!" to some member of your family and you were told in no uncertain terms that your mouth would be washed out with soap if those feelings were expressed again? Have you ever in anger yelled out, "I wish you were dead!" and an unspoken glare of violent disapproval warned you that those feelings would not be tolerated? Were you ever terrified by thunder or lightning or by the dark? Maybe you cried or shook from fear as you were told, "A big boy is never afraid!" Did you ever say that it made you feel good all over to be touched by someone and you were told that you should be ashamed of ever having such a feeling?

Have you ever been in someone's living room with a small group of people when you no longer heard the words but were appalled by the jealousy, the hate, the resentment, the mass of ill will coming out in the conversation? Yet did you get the impression that everyone else was concentrating on the words, because we have been taught to pay close attention to people's words? To some people, conversation is an umbrella for hiding true feelings and thoughts, even if they use the word *feeling* in their talk. The language of saying simply and naturally what is in our hearts is at least as difficult to learn as Chinese or Swahili and takes as much practice.

Words count a lot in our country. We put a lot of stock in them and invest a lot of time on them. How well we use words is a mark of our education. Being very time-oriented and purpose-minded, most of us feel that spending time on studying ourselves, our feelings, is not accomplishing anything and is not an achievement. Success in the form of achievement, performance, conformity is what many Americans consider important to aim for. Our schools reflect this thinking by striving to develop the so-called objective thinker, devoid of emotional involvement, guided only by logic, supported by quantitative evidence, a vast accumulation of facts, aided by a jetlike rapidity of response and an enviable precision of delivery.

There is much in this that is worthy and necessary for training people to live in our country now and in the future, but are we not also educating ourselves out of our feelings, away from ourselves? Objective thinking at its best is based not only on marshaling known facts and scientific truths, but also on recognizing and dealing with feelings. Almost all our behavior is motivated by feelings. Far too often the tranquil voice of reason is overpowered by the shrill cries of the terrorized child still lodged within the adult. Are we not more competent to employ reason and logic when we are in touch with our feelings?

There is a purpose in all our behavior. There is a meaning to everything we do, every way we act, everything we say. All of us say at times, "Oh, it just happened that way," but it happened for a reason, a reason that we may never know or want to know or need to know. We cannot and should not try to understand every facet of our lives, but our feelings do count, and there are times when we need to take an inventory of our feelings so that we can act with more reason and logic.

In the course of giving aid to industrially less developed countries, our government has gradually learned that the way people *feel* about receiving the aid is important, that the aid has to be wanted by the people and cannot be superimposed on them if it is to help. For example, a land-reform program cannot be made to work simply because the authorities desire it. The population must be ready to change and fundamentally sympathetic with the purpose behind the reform. If the people in X country feel strongly about something, no amount of logic, evidence, reason, machinery, or money is going to change their feelings fundamentally and produce successful innovation. Aid that interferes with the traditions and meaningful social patterns of a people can boomerang, for the feelings of the people must be taken into consideration and respected in order to ensure their cooperation. What our government has learned is something each of us must learn.

Feelings enter into all our relationships. Feelings rarely revealed or even recognized by us can influence our choice of careers or marriage partners. Feelings that perhaps we are not tuned in on can cause our liking for one thing, our avoidance of another, our confusion about something else. We may be able to enumerate more than eight logical reasons why we came to a certain decision, but that does not necessarily mean that our feelings did not bring about the decision. A personnel officer can sometimes find many so-called objective reasons why he did not hire a highly qualified person, but upon reflection he might find that the person's face reminded him of someone important in his life whom he disliked intensely. When several of us hear some-one talk and we explore later what each one heard, we find that each of us heard something different, although the main thread of what the person said may run through all our accounts. What we hear and what we see are colored by our experiences and feelings.

There are feelings that we know we have, that we are conscious of having. Some people know their signals better than others, but no one is conscious of his every feeling. There is a vast expanse of feelings tucked away in secret corners of ourselves that are out of our awareness, hidden forces that cause us to do things. They come out in curious ways. Have you ever been surprised yourself at the violence of your response to a simple question that may be a form of chitchat? "How is your mother?" said a girl to a boy whose family she had met once, and the boy heard himself spitting out, "What's it to you! Are you a mother-lover or something?" That response was way out of proportion to the question and quite inappropriate. But the question may have ignited feelings that had been carefully stored somewhere down under and they burst forth. These are meaningful signals that point up the need for this boy to do some exploration and probing into the recesses of his relationships with his parents, some uncovering of incidents he may have temporarily forgotten.

There is meaning in what we forget as well as in what we remember. Have you ever completely forgotten about an appointment you made? Most of us have. If we actively pursue our forgetfulness and discard myriads of external reasons why we didn't show up at an appointment, we are likely to discover that something in that situation made us feel uncomfortable. Whether we knew it or not, down deep we wanted to avoid that situation and avoid being uncomfortable. Perhaps you forgot to invite a friend to your party; did you really want her there in the first place, or did it just happen that you forgot?

We all forget things, appointments, people, and we all occasionally make slips of the tongue or the pen. We may be writing a letter—suddenly certain words appear on the paper as if the pen wrote them by itself. What magic! But what kind of magic causes you to be terribly embarrassed when you mean to say one thing and something else comes popping right out of your mouth? The magic is the language of our feelings creeping out from under our control.

Dreams are another part of this revealing language. All over the world people dream. Some people dream more than others, some remember more of their dreams than others. The drama, the form, the style, the movements, the words, and the significance of these change from person to person, country to country. Our dreams—yes, even the ones that seem wildly absurd and bizarre—have meaning. They give us clues to our true feelings. Our dreams are communication systems flashing messages to ourselves.

What are dreams made of? Not sugar and spice and everything nice, but the sum total of all our experiences and feelings. Our most painful moments, as well as our most pleasurable ones, appear in disguised forms, so distorted, exaggerated, and symbolic that we are often at a loss to appreciate their particular meanings to us. The secrets of our innermost life that we may never have reckoned with appear in our dreams.

When we are disturbed by a remembered dream, that is a signal for us to take notice. The second step is to try to think out what the dream or the upset feeling it provokes relates to—something that happened yesterday or many yesterdays back. Dreams can refer back to earliest childhood experiences that in our wakeful moments we have completely forgotten. The unrecognized, rarely revealed feelings that are expressed in dreams, in forgetting, in slips of the tongue and the pen are really quite subversive. These feelings can be troublemakers for us. They make for unrest, upset the outward calm, challenge the status quo. Investigation is required and is often very helpful in creating peace within ourselves.

The language of our feelings is also expressed by our movement. Have you ever noticed that you move one way when you are feeling content and satisfied and you move another way when you are depressed? Our bodies express our feelings not only through the ways we move but also through our state of health. Have you ever remarked how strange a coincidence it was that you had a terrible cold on an exam day or that you felt sick to your stomach when you were frightened by something?

Our feelings, when working overtime within us, can produce illnesses that are just as intense in pain or discomfort as a contagious disease. Many of our everyday expressions indicate the influence our feelings have over our bodily processes:

I am sick and tired of that.
She gives me a pain in the neck.
He wanted to get it off his chest.
I'm not going to let them give me ulcers.
It makes me want to throw up.
Oh, my aching back, when will he shut up?
I could feel my fever rise.
Listening to her gives me a headache.
Don't get your bowels in such an uproar over that!
I've had enough of your bellyaching.

Surely you can add a list of your own to these examples.

When we are disturbed or unhappy about something, our feelings signal us in many different ways. Some of us get sick. Some get sleepy. Some dream a lot. Some eat a lot. Some drink a lot. Some "sex" a lot. Some "take a fix." Some keep violently busy. Some of us get lost in a crowd or bury ourselves in a book or glue ourselves to the television set. Some people take it out on other people.

Is there anything wrong with extra sleeping, eating, drinking, or overindulging in any activity? Sometimes a person can get over a difficult period by these means, creating a protective insulation of a sort. None of us is perfect, and there are times when even the most self-aware person finds himself trying to escape his problems in ways basically not destructive to others or himself. On the other hand, when these escape routes become our way of dealing with all reverses and with even the slightest hint of difficulties, we are thrust deeper into the grip of our uncomfortable feelings. These feelings, in turn, can tyrannize us. This tyranny is destructive to us and often to others. Just like the slip of the pen that magically seems to write some words on paper, the feelings that lie behind the escape routes seem to take us over. We are thrust further along our escape routes, be they eating, drinking, drugs, sex, sleep, illness, isolation, busyness, aggression, and we are thereby ruled more and more by our ungoverned feelings.

The man who cannot hold a job, the woman who constantly redecorates her home and her children, the boy who loses his homework daily, the girl who is involved in one accident after another—all are in the clutches of their feelings. A pattern of the same thing happening to the same person is more than chance; it is an indication that certain feelings at work inside are begging for recognition and exploration.

The more we disregard our feelings,
the more we suppress our feelings,
the more uncertain we become of our feelings,
the more those feelings cling to us.

The more those feelings creep out to express themselves,
the more we are governed by feelings we no longer recognize.

Hate, fear, envy, guilt, lust—none of these can be so
dreadful and damaging unless allowed some damaging form
of expression. If we recognize the feelings, we can limit their
expression and sometimes even direct them into constructive channels. We are tyrannized by these feelings when
we shelve them in locked compartments away from ourselves and throw away the keys.

If feelings that go back to the yesterdays of our childhood
control, govern, tyrannize us, we may find ourselves treating
all colleagues as we did the brother whom we envied, leaning
excessively upon all teachers as we did on our mothers, or
fearing all employers and officials as we feared our fathers.
We can change somewhat the cycle of these relationships
with the sharp tool of insight. As we dig deep to remember, struggle not to forget, increase our awareness of our
previous and early relationships and the powerful influence
they have on us, then our future relationships with colleagues, teachers, employers, and officials can change. The
awareness that, hopefully, we develop over the years changes
not only our relationships with others but also our feelings
about ourselves.

Our parents give us a feeling about ourselves. How our
parents felt they felt about us and how we felt they felt
about us may be two different stories, but our picture of
ourselves grows out of our family's camera.

If as children we felt prized by our parents, we received
the encouragement to have a greater sense of our own personal worth. If we were looked upon as bad, or even felt
we were looked upon as bad, we are likely to feel worthless.
If we feel like worms, we squirm through life.

The girl who feels she is bad and worthless may spend her whole life trying to prove her worth to everyone through a dazzling career, or she may set out to prove just how bad she really is. If she gets into trouble with the law, that may convince her that she *is* bad, and a criminal career could begin. The boy who feels unloved and unlovable may spend his whole life avoiding close contact with anyone by withdrawing into private alleys or immersing himself in so many crowds that no single relationship is meaningful. Have you ever met a person who has a nasty word for everyone? You can be sure that that person does not like himself and is just as intolerant of himself as he is of others.

One of the hardest things in life is to be able to accept our own shortcomings, poor judgment, and physical and emotional clumsiness yet still believe that we are nice and worthwhile. Accepting our own shortcomings helps us accept the imperfections of others. There is no perfect person, just as there is no perfect parent, just as there is no perfect child, just as there is no perfect world.

In all our relationships, we are influenced by our feelings. How we feel about ourselves strongly influences how we feel about others, which largely reflects how we feel about ourselves. Our feelings are powerful signals that can damage our lives and that can protect and help our lives. The feelings behind the words, the feelings behind the actions—these are the signals we need to recognize and decipher, these need the most attention.

3. *Fear*

WHAT IS FEAR? It is a feeling. It is a signal. We feel some kind of danger when we experience fear. It is uncomfortable. Fear is a discomfort that varies in degree from a mild, nebulous, unsafe feeling to one of such intensity that we are ready to push the panic button. Real or imagined, reasonable or unreasonable, appropriate or inappropriate, we feel this discomfort called fear. Here are some of the things we say about fear in our daily conversations:

I'm frightened to death!
She is scared stiff.
He is scared silly.
She is laughing hysterically, she is so scared.
That child is trembling with fear.
They are scared speechless.
My heart is pounding with fear!
I was so scared I nearly wet my pants.
That scared me so much I clutched the nearest person.
I had chills running up and down my spine.
His blood pressure hit the ceiling, he was so frightened.
She is even frightened by her own shadow.

Fear probes deep within us, and it springs from depths within us. We don't only fear with our minds, with our thought processes. The expressions we use about fear demonstrate that we fear with our bodies as well. Fear reaches down to our fingertips and toes. Fear can raise our blood pressure, increase our pulse rate, quicken our heartbeat, and pour adrenaline into our systems at such a rapid rate that we are capable of an inordinate amount of strength. The way we breathe is affected by how frightened we are. The way we walk, the way we talk, and certainly the way we act are affected by fear.

Fear springs from experiences we have had that made us feel unsafe and threatened. We learn and feel fear early in our lives. Parents usually teach little children to recognize what they should be afraid of in order to protect their lives. ("Don't touch the stove." "Don't run into the street." "Be careful of knives.") Also, unknowingly, they transmit their own set of fears to their children, fears which may not necessarily be useful for protecting children from hazards. Their fears are catching. Also, we create our own private fears out of our experiences and imagination. Normally, as we grow older, we gradually acquire the judgment to recognize when we should be afraid, when something is hazardous. In addition, we learn to distinguish between real and imagined fears. We slowly separate out the fears that are appropriate to the situation—reasonable fears—and the fears that are not appropriate to the situation—unreasonable fears. We can make judgments on the basis of the fears we know and understand.

Often we are doing this without even realizing we are doing it, because often we do not understand some of our fears or really think about them. Fear serves a purpose in our lives. A certain degree of fear is useful to us. An overabundance of fear just as a complete lack of fear can endanger our lives.

Fear is a danger signal. "Watch out!" we are warned by the knowing wonders inside us. As unsafe and threatened as fear can make us feel, it can and it has protected us. Mankind could not have developed if we had not known and feared starvation, wild animals, falling off a cliff, getting run over, being burned by fire, and a whole host of other things. Fear, the danger signal essential to our survival, has repeated its warnings over the centuries to *stop, look, listen, think, take stock, change, act*—and we have not given it much credit for that!

Have you ever wondered about the many things in this world we have good reason to fear? Have you ever thought of the many potentially dangerous forces in nature and society that can harm us and lead to fear? Fear of fire, drought, and lightning, fear of cold, starvation, and disease forced early man to set up life so that he could be protected. Early man realized also that ignorance was his enemy. Through being afraid, early man learned to channel his fears into constructive patterns of action that helped him survive, prosper, progress. Early man learned that fire could do more than burn and harm him—fire could keep him warm, could be used for cooking, for signaling friends, and for warding away enemies. Although still aware of the real danger of fire and its power of destroying lives and homes, he was no longer terrified of fire, because he had found ways to use it positively, and he could master it.

The drive to survive is a strong life force within us. For most of us, life is precious, and the thrills and joys of living compensate for the frustrations and ordeals. But sometimes when life gets tough, all of us, to one degree or another, flirt with thoughts about death. Death is an escape route for us from pain and unhappiness; at the same time, it can serve as punishment for those we think have inflicted this unhappiness upon us. "How they will suffer for their sins!" we like to think. Remember the line in the song "Old Man River" about being tired of living, yet afraid of dying? This expresses feelings common to many of us. Unlike the animals, who cannot reason as we do, we know from an early age that eventually we shall die, that death is inevitable and a mystery. Little children explore this subject and crave for reassurance that they will not be deserted. It is natural for us to have some fears about dying. It is also natural for us to want to create as many ways as possible to prolong our lives and to invent new ideas to assuage our fears. If this is true, why has man through the centuries been involved in destruction and wars?

We have sheltered ourselves in groups to protect ourselves from real, and sometimes from imagined, fears. There is strength in numbers, and the person who feels weak and helpless alone often feels strong in a group. Groups, clubs, fraternities, gangs can help assuage our fears. Often it is fear and the need for support that lead many racial, religious, and national groups to develop strong contacts with each other.

The family, our oldest institution, is nature's way of a built-in protection. The family has existed in one form or another since the beginning of the world, proving its resilience and strength as an institution and our need for it. The family grew into larger families, tribes, clans, communities, and societies. There was safety, comfort in numbers. Besides, the family gives the helpless, dependent baby the props and support he needs to develop into an independent person. The family provides for close, dependable relationships, for a comfortable secure base where presumably *people who care* help children grow into the finest human beings possible. The family, with all the conflicts that normally arise within it, seems to be the most effective institution yet devised by the world for the protection, care, and raising of children. Religious groups recognize the fundamental importance of family to mankind. One expression of this is how the Catholics title their religious and clergy—Mother Superior, Father, Sister, Brother.

A sense of trust is developed in the first year of life. The repeated experience of being hungry, receiving the food, feeling relieved from the frustration of want, being comforted by the fulfillment of a need is the main source of an infant's assurance that the world is a dependable place. Our distrust is also formed in the cradle, and later events tend to strengthen or weaken that distrust. If a baby is hungry and does not receive food or enough of it or not soon enough or does not feel comforted or relieved, then he is frustrated, angry, and fearful.

Babies, as helpless and completely dependent upon their parents as they are, come into the world with a strong life force. It is amazing how much faulty handling they can weather. They are tough. Love, like food, is basic to their survival. Children have been known to die for lack of either. Pediatricians and psychiatrists in children's hospitals are all familiar with the baby who fails to gain weight or who is apathetic and depressed as a result of not enough love and proper mothering. The usual therapeutic measure for this consists of an around-the-clock nurse, a consistent and constant mother substitute for the baby. After a few weeks of this, the baby has dramatically improved, weight has increased enormously, apathy has been replaced by alertness and responsiveness. The baby has responded to the love given to him and now has something to live for.

Have you ever visited an orphanage or a children's village and had the children race up to you or sneak up behind you just to touch you? A visitor to one large institution remarked sadly, "If only I could have touched each one of the children, a little hug, a parting embrace, even a clasp of the hand, I would have felt I had done something useful today."

Beginning earlier than we think, infants fear desertion, and they fear losing their parents' love and approval. A little one's fears can be reassured by Mother or Father just being there, by a hug and a kiss, a loving pat on the back, by a feeling of being able to count on someone. A strong protective arm around the shoulder can give a child a stronger feeling of safety than the prettiest choice of words. Touch is often a more powerful reassurance than sight or sound to the littlest child, as well as to the adult. Hasn't that been true in your experience?

An attitude of indifference and neglect toward children on the part of parents just increases the fears of children, produces anger, and further increases the fears of the children and their parents. When a child is not given an opportunity to express his fears, or when adults scold or tease him for being afraid, the fears plunge down deeper. There is an upsurge of guilt feelings—feeling guilty for being afraid. Children have many fears. It is part of growing up and part of life to have them. How fears were treated in our childhood and how we handled them can set the tone for how we handle fears throughout our lives.

It is not uncommon or necessarily an indication of something unhealthy for little children to be afraid of the dark, of water, of loud noises, of drain pipes and big machines, of animals and heights. The degree and duration of the fear is the clue to determine whether it is unhealthy. In a country that emphasizes bigness and strength, children are abundantly aware that they are little and dependent upon big people for their survival. Often little ones are terrified by midgets in the circus, perhaps because the midgets emphasize to them their own smallness and bring out a fear that they might not grow up the way they want to. They fear abnormality, which is part of the morbid curiosity that they have about all people with defects.

At some time in his life, nearly every child is awed by and fearful of a giant, and why not? Grownups seem like giants to them, and the grown-up giants set limits, requirements, and demand a certain amount of obedience. Sometimes children "conquer" the giants through play, fantasies, and dreams. They climb to the top of the jungle gym and feel above it all. They pretend they are policemen, soldiers, and other figures of power and authority. They construct wars where the "little people" find all kinds of clever ways to outtrick and destroy the giants. Children adore the cartoon features that have the clever little mouse making a clumsy fool out of the big, slow elephant; they enjoy reading about little David vanquishing giant Goliath and seeing Dennis the Menace making life uncomfortable for the oldsters.

Some children carry the fear of giants into adulthood with them. They still look upon the giants as omnipotent, all-powerful, and threatening. They go through life feeling small and powerless. Most of us fortunately come to the realization, gradually, that our parents or parent substitutes (usually the giants in our lives) are human beings who have limitations, make mistakes, and are not so overpowering and threatening as we may have once felt. But some of us carry our giants along a lifetime route laid with the fears of yesterday. Then we tend to pick up all sorts of new ones along the way to obstruct our progress. This route weakens our confidence in ourselves, which makes it harder for us to overcome the obstacles of society that may come before us. The person who feels hopeless about himself as a person is reinforced in this fear if he is also a victim of prejudice, poverty, or deprived in any other way. Being of a minority race or religion or being economically underprivileged or being handicapped physically or mentally is so much harder if we fear that basically we are "no good."

Our relationships with others are complicated by fear. A close attachment to our parents or to some adult in or out of the family is our life line. Any threat to this makes us fear for our survival. When a younger brother or sister appears in our lives, there is a threat to our security. A child's jealousy of rivals is as natural as his need for his mother. A certain amount of jealousy is inevitable. Have you tended to believe that jealousy was always bad and unnatural? A lot of people look on it this way. But jealousy is often a form of testing.

It is not only the schools that are expert at testing. Children from a very early age are experts at testing first their parents and later others. What are they testing? Children are testing to reaffirm that their parents still love them, that they count, that they are important to their parents. When a new brother or sister appears or whenever children think or feel that there is some threat in their relationship with their parents, when they feel shaky in that love, it can be fully expected that their skills in testing will be put to active use to reassure themselves that everything is O.K.

A child especially tests his parents to make sure he is still loved when there is an introduction of a rival in the family, one of those adorable, cute, pink-cheeked babies that can scare an older child to pieces. The older child's feeling of reassurance depends on his parents' action and reactions far

more than their words. Since parents react and act so differently with each child as a result of what is going on in their
lives internally and externally at the time of the arrival of
each child, we can safely say that each child, in effect, has
a different set of parents. Each child is treated differently
from all others, no matter how large or small the family.
Each has different experiences with the parents, each reacts
differently in his relationship with his parents and usually
is looked upon as a unique person in his own right. We
might say that each child in his unique relationship with his
parents would like to have his parents all to himself.

The child tests his parents by demanding extra attention.
Parents give the attention through reassurance when necessary or through scolding and reprimands when necessary.
Children often purposely do things that are "naughty," for
this is one of the ways they can receive attention, and even
negative attention or a spanking is better than no attention.

Woven into the testing process of the child are fears—
fear of loss of love, fear of loss of approval, fear of loss of
recognition and status, and fears about the child's own
negative feelings. Let us look at a two-and-half-year-old
girl who has been an only child in her family until her little
brother arrives. Even though her parents may have prepared
her well for this, she quickly comes to see this little brother
as a rival and a threat to her receiving from her parents the
attention, the care, and the love she is used to. She fears her
position in the family has been usurped. Perhaps she plays
with some nasty thoughts about how she can get rid of this
rival or hurt him. She is often frightened by her own
thoughts. What is going on inside her is not always obvious.
She may be open about her negative feelings and give little
brother a good swift smack in full view of everybody, or she
may ask her parents to take him back where he came from.

She may hug little brother to "death" or take sneaky little swipes at him while cooing at him when elders are around, or she may submerge her negative feelings entirely and suppress any actions toward him. No matter how she tries to hide these feelings, they remain strong within her. These feelings and reactions affect her future relationships in all areas of life.

Chances are that she never plots this out or decides knowingly that, on the basis of her feelings about her little brother, she will act in such and such a way. It all happens because our relationships with others are influenced by the relationships established in our childhood, the relationships with our parents being a strong determinant of all our later relationships. Can you see any similarity in the way you treat your sisters and brothers, your parents, your teachers and in the way you act with your friends and acquaintances?

Do you think there may have been times when you thought you were adopted (when you were not) or unloved by your parents (when you were not) just because they seemed to pay more attention to someone else in your family? Most of us have had these fantasies that are based on our fears of being deserted by the people we depend on so much.

Love, like food, can be shared if we feel there is enough to go around. We have to feel sure that we will not be left out. When we fear a scarcity of these things, when we feel deprived, often we push others or try to push others out of the way to make sure we have enough for ourselves. We are angry at others for "horning in." Sometimes we are angry at ourselves for pushing, and we end up fearing both retaliation and more deprivation. Greed and envy are based on fear.

We all fear war and destruction. It is related not only to

our desire for survival—the real fear of being destroyed, mutilated, or harmed—but also to fears concerning retaliation. All of us share a desire for peace in the world; but peace begins in the family, because that is where most wars start—and some never end. Conflicts are part of family living. The fear, the anger, and the guilt feelings that accompany many conflicts are feelings we all experience and must learn to cope with. We develop a lot of fears in the training ground of the family, and we learn ways to take care of or control our fears in the same place. The family is a training ground, a communication center, and, to some extent, a control center. Hopefully, we learn useful ways within our families to meet fears and resolve conflicts by being helped to build the strongest fortress against fears— self-confidence. Self-confidence, a feeling of our own intrinsic worth—this is what families can help give above all else. And what counts more?

When a family does not encourage a feeling of self-confidence in a child, then fear flourishes. How does the fear display itself? Each person expresses his fears differently. Some of us engage in persistent and seemingly unnecessary lying and cheating. The child who feels self-confident feels a greater assurance in telling the truth about his misdeeds to his parents and accepting the consequences. A child can even disagree with his parents if he is not pervaded by fear. Learning respectfully to disagree face to face with one's parents, to attempt to resolve the disagreements with one's parents, may be the essence of democracy. Democracy relies on each person's feeling of personal worth, on his ability to make choices as well as to accept them, to question, and to participate responsibly in creating better conditions. Democracy depends upon the ability of each one of us to meet our fears and work them out construc-

Peace begins in the family, because that is where most wars start—and some never end.

tively, rather than letting our fears govern us, harming both ourselves and others.

When fears are not met by us, they increase and apply pressure within that leads to more conflict. More conflict can become explosive and can lead to angry actions and the shooting off of our mouths or guns. Therefore, fear can produce wars. Fear can produce wars inside ourselves, in our families, in our nation, and in the world. An overpopulated country fearful of not having enough food or enough land for its people to develop healthfully may declare war on a neighboring country. A nation defeated in one war—and, as a result, lacking in confidence and questioning its own worth and significance—may try to make its people more amenable to another war. In this context, it becomes easier to understand how a Hitler could slowly take over a nation by playing upon its great fears. One of the main Nazi songs expresses this idea. It began:

Holy Fatherland in danger, thy sons gather round thee,
Encircled by danger,
Holy Fatherland we all stand together hand in hand.

It becomes clear that an outside pressure of fear—real or imagined—can produce anger in people and can encourage banding together in self-defense against real or imagined injustice. This unity gives a sense of common purpose as well as a temporary inner release from the potent feelings of fear, anger, and guilt. However, collective action can also prevent war.

When the western European nations feared the Russians, they joined the United States in setting up NATO as a collective security measure to be a bulwark against the USSR, to calm the fears of their nations, and to avoid war and destruction if possible. If a school has poor standards, an inadequate building, and inadequate teachers, a group of parents collectively can often bring about corrective action based on their fears that their children will receive a poor education. And if a group of white people want to keep a Negro family out of a neighborhood or if a group of Protestants want to keep Jews or Catholics out of a neighborhood, we have seen that collective action unfortunately can often accomplish this too. President Franklin Delano Roosevelt learned the truth about fear, for he recognized its usefulness as a protection to us. But he also understood its potentialities for destruction when he eloquently cautioned that "the only thing we have to fear is fear itself."

Separating out the fears that are appropriate to a situation and can protect us—reasonable fears—from those that come out of a wellspring of other experiences and are not appropriate to the particular situation and can harm us—unreasonable fears—is a life task for all of us. Those of us who can face fear with our eyes wide open can usually choose paths of action most helpful and least harmful to ourselves and to those around us. This takes guts! It takes an inner strength that springs from the lonely depths within, where fears linger. A person can survive almost anything if he can survive his fears.

Have you ever suffered while thinking about a coming doctor's appointment, worrying about it, fearing it, imagining all kinds of fascinatingly awful diseases you could have, and then you went to the appointment and it was not at all what you feared? The hours of fearing, worrying, and anticipating the worst are usually far more painful than the visit itself. How often have you sweated through a few days before a date and experienced that funny feeling in your stomach and those cold, clammy hands as the time drew closer? If you have been in an awful automobile accident with a bad driver, isn't it natural for you to fear driving with him again? How about ghosts and shadows, do they frighten you? Should they?

The advertisements we read, hear, and see often set off and rocket our fears about ourselves. The ads tell us we won't have body odor or halitosis if we use such and such a product, so we are afraid that maybe we smell and are therefore unacceptable to others. They play on any fears of ugliness we may have, and they make it clear that we can hide our ugliness by employing some kind of cream, powder, or make-up. They lead us to understand that people will like us better if we are dressed a certain way or have our hair styled a special way. They lead us to fear the aging process—the wrinkles, the gray hair, the arthritis, the fatigue. The ads emphasize that men who are 100 per cent masculine and women who are 100 per cent feminine use their product. There are even ads that imply that you might not get married if you do not use certain products. These ads don't create fears, but they can provide a thrust that strengthens our dormant fears about ourselves.

What the ads play on to sell their products are our fears about ourselves. They choose fears common to all of us. Research has been done by various companies on what fears are common to all of us. They know it is normal for us to have many fears. But how they use this knowledge can be harmful at times. However, there is some reassurance in knowing that we share many fears. What fears do we share? The following are some common fears:

fears of physical danger to our survival
fears of not being loved, approved of, appreciated
fears of failure

fears of not doing well enough
fears of losing face with family and friends
fears of not being attractive enough
fears of abnormality
fears of not being sexually attractive
fears of not being accepted by friends
fears of not being liked
fears of discrimination
fears of loss of control
fears of not being feminine enough
fears of not being masculine enough
fears of being overdeveloped or underdeveloped
fears of intercourse
fears of pregnancy
fears of venereal disease
fears of mutilation
fears of unpleasant body odor
fears of disagreement
fears of flunking out of school
fears of not getting married
fears of not finding or holding a job
fears of not being a worthwhile person

The degree to which fears affect, control, immobilize, or change our lives is what determines whether they are within the realm of normality or not. If you are clean and your fear of body odor causes you to wash every five minutes, then that fear has taken on unreasonable proportions—for reasons that need exploration. If a fear of failure predominates in your life and every experience, every relationship threatens to be a failure, then the fear has become unreasonable. If an attractive girl is afraid she is unattractive and becomes "loose" with the boys of the neighborhood to prove to herself and others that she is attractive, then her fears about herself are in the driver's seat. If a boy is attractive to girls but his fears about whether he is masculine enough upset him so much that he avoids all girls, then his fears are isolating him from half the world. It is remarkable how often a little exploration into the heart's pocket can pull out some fears that we can take a good look at, deal with, and relieve, so they don't govern our actions.

The boy who is afraid that he is not masculine enough, who is worried about his masculinity, naturally has to find ways to comfort himself and find relief from his fears. Isolating himself from girls, as mentioned before, is one way. But there are many other ways, such as assuming a tough pose, talking big, being a bully, telling vulgar jokes, carrying weapons, being overly sexually aggressive with girls. Some men involved in assault, rape, or gunplay incidents are trying, among other things, to prove their masculinity. The attractive girl who feels unattractive, who is worried about her adequacy as a female, may be "loose" with boys or may withdraw from contact with boys. She may become excessively competitive with boys, perhaps to the extent that she wishes she were a boy. She may have difficulties with girl friends, and as with a boy, she may participate in what is considered delinquent behavior because of her fears about herself.

All of us experience a certain amount of fear before taking an exam, particularly if the test means passing a course, getting a job, getting into college. It is natural for us to have a certain amount of apprehension about something unknown, and a test is an unknown quantity. It is also natural for us to fear that we do not know enough. Does any human being know enough? It is inevitable that we worry about what will happen if we do not pass a big test. What do we do when we are afraid we won't pass a test? Some of us freeze into inaction; some of us push the fear out of our minds and start to quake only when we walk into the examination room; some of us put a protective covering over the fear with a "so-what-if I-don't-pass" attitude; some of us sleep an inordinate amount; some drink or eat more; and often we get sick from fear.

Does it help to peer at our fear of the coming test? It is reassuring to know most people are afraid of tests. If we know that we are scared, and it is reasonable to be so, we can then explore what is at stake for us when we take the exam. One obvious way of dealing with this fear is to study more for the test so that we are on top of the material and can do as well as we are able. If we don't do that, a few searching probes into "why not" are in order.

But then there are many of us who do study a lot or who are extraordinarily bright and talented who invariably do poorly on tests and whose fear is way out of proportion to the test situation. Some of us thrive on, and some of us are completely demoralized by, competition and pressured situations. Could it be that a test situation is part of a scoring process that has threatened us since we were tiny? Could it be that we often glorify a test to signify proof of our worthiness or unworthiness as a person? Could it be that we fear that our low opinion of ourselves will be confirmed by a low test score? Our fear of tests is marked by a lack of self-confidence. Too often we rate ourselves by our test scores (and so do some teachers and parents, unfortunately), and that is a tenuous way to live.

When we avoid fear, we travel along routes littered with discomfort, unhappinesses, and doubt. Many good times, good friends, achievements, satisfactions, and thrills are missed when fear that has been pushed aside gets too strong a grip on us. When we walk straight up to fear, respect it, question it, then usually we can do something positive about it. We can at least relieve our discomfort. Often we can change the situation or change our attitude toward the situation. If we cannot cope with it alone, we can turn to someone we trust to help us.

Our fears are valuable danger signals warning us to take heed and tune in.

Fear of things we understand and know—reasonable fear—is so much easier to deal with than unlabeled feelings of fear. When we don't know what we are afraid of, this is an awful experience. We all share a dislike for not knowing what is going on, that queasy feeling of confusion, doubt, and puzzlement. When we are afraid of forces that we do not understand, frequently we protect ourselves with rituals, superstitions, magic, and dogma to relieve our fears. The Pueblo Indians, a very close-knit group of people who live mostly in the Southwest, fear not having enough rain, because then they will not have enough food to live. Their survival is as dependent upon the unity they have created within their society as it is upon the rain without. The rites of the Pueblo religion are built around a belief in the supernatural and, when given the necessary observance, ensure rain, rich crops, and other blessings. They pray for rain, they dance for rain, they chant for rain, and they employ other rituals to deal with this unpredictable force. If there is enough rain, they feel that their prayers brought it about; and if there is not enough rain, they may fear that they did not pray enough or that the forces of evil were too strong. When we don't understand something, such as what brings on rain and how to protect crops without rain, fear is prevalent. As ignorance is gradually supplanted by knowledge, overwhelming fear takes on new proportions and is more amenable to change.

Parents deal constantly with the unknown. Each child is an unknown. Each child is a unique personality. There are no set formulas, no instant miracles, no ready-mixed capsules that parents can produce to use with a child. Conscientious parents, and this embraces most parents, often fear their own inadequacies as parents. Magazine articles, certain books, TV, movies, advertisements do not dispel their fears but encourage them. "Where have I failed with you?" "I wish I could make you happier." "What have I done to cause you to act like this?" "If only I knew . . ." These comments of parents, and many more, reflect parents' fears of inadequacy. As parents grow older and become grandparents and senior citizens, they fear they may be useless to their children and society, and they continue to fear their inadequacies to one degree or another.

It seems that we are never too young or too old, too small or too big to be afraid. Is that why the age-old adage of parents is "don't be afraid"? Perhaps parents are reassuring themselves by warning their children not to be afraid. Think of some of the admonitions you have received about fear from your parents, teachers, doctors, and even friends: "It is childish to give in to your fears." "You are too big to be afraid." "Only sissies are afraid." "Don't be a scaredycat."

We often tend to treat fears with a positive disrespect. We act as if it is unhealthy, unnatural, bad, and useless to have fears, when it is often just the opposite. Many of us doubt our value and worth as human beings, many of us worry too much about how others value us; we think we have to appear strong to please others, for to show fear is a sign of weakness, and we don't want to be weak. *Therefore, many people are afraid to be afraid.*

4. Anger

BOY, WAS I ANGRY!
She makes me see red.
I turned purple with rage.
He turned white with anger.
They were blind with rage.
I was so angry I couldn't see straight.
The feeling of anger colors the way we see life.

Dad had a fit.
Mother almost burst a blood vessel.
You could see his back arch.
She was so angry, she could not open her mouth.
He nearly burst his appendix. His ulcer got worked up.
Her nostrils quivered with anger. His eyes spit blood.
His body was shaking and his fists were clenched in anger.
The powerful feeling of anger can often affect the way our
bodies function.

I could have killed her, I was so angry.
He attacked her in rage.
Mother hit the ceiling.
Dad was so mad he could have spit nails.

He was fit to be tied.
I was so angry I could have skinned a cat.
He could have broken every bone in her body.
She nearly burst her buttons with rage.
I could have kicked her teeth in.
The teacher blew her stack. She fumed. She was boiling up.
She was on fire. She was sizzling with anger. She blew up.
I exploded with anger.
Anger is an explosive feeling.

Look at the rather violent ways we blast off about these feelings in our daily conversations. We use words like *mad, enraged, furious, annoyed, hostile, irritated, livid* to describe varying aspects of anger. We talk a lot about anger, for anger is a feeling all of us know.

Anger is primarily the result of keenly felt injustice, whether this injustice is imagined or real. Anger is a signal that we feel frustrated, hurt, or betrayed by others. It is a flashing, red-hot signal that profoundly affects our lives. Many of us have been burned by anger, and there are times when it has destroyed some of our relationships. That we all get angry at times is understandable and O.K., but how we handle our angry feelings is the burning issue.

Our anger is caused by "notted" feelings:

not being loved, wanted, approved of
not being accepted for ourselves
not being listened to
not being able to depend on anyone
not being left alone
not being included, understood, needed, believed, trusted
not feeling safe, secure, free
not feeling able, capable, good

not feeling close to others
not getting attention, response, fair treatment
not getting credit, recognition
not getting what we want
not having a sense of belonging
not having enough of the necessities of life
not having opportunities to do what we want
not having the chance to develop ourselves to the fullest

You know these "nots," which can tie us up in knots. You can add a few of your own. These "nots" are first tied in the family.

Our first rewards, along with our first frustrations, occur in family life. From infancy on, it is our parents, our sisters, and our brothers who are usually most capable of inciting our anger. None of us is born angry. We are not possessed by devils as was once believed. None of us grows up angry as a result of supernatural forces. There is nothing magical about anger. There are times when we would like to believe this, just as we might prefer to stick pins in voodoo dolls or effigies of people we are angry with rather than working out our feelings about them. We are usually most angry at the people we depend upon the most, because they are the ones who can disappoint us and hurt us the most and, as a result, are the ones whom we wish to please the most and alienate the least. We are most angry when we care most deeply about someone—or something.

In order to expose true feelings, we have to feel safe in a relationship. When we feel safe with someone, we know that an occasional outburst of anger will not severely alter the relationship. If our relationship with someone is shaky and we do not feel safe with that person, chances are that we squelch the anger that we feel and express it in less direct ways that are not satisfying in the long run. Often we feel trapped by these indirect methods, and we all know that nothing gets us angrier than the feeling of being trapped.

As with fear, anger can protect us and help us achieve more satisfying lives. The baby's screams of anger usually bring an adult who gives the food and the attention that is needed. A young person's anger at unfair treatment, such as being falsely accused by a teacher of doing something wrong, can often bring about fairer treatment through open discussion. An adult's anger at something that goes against his principles can often lead to reforms. A country's anger at having to submit to unjust colonialism can lead to independence and freedom for that country.

Since we are normally born with built-in signals that are for our own protection, we cannot ignore these signals. We must learn to use our built-in signals, such as anger, in such a way that they do protect us and do not harm others. It is normal, reasonable, appropriate, and inevitable for us to feel angry at times. This is what we so often overlook. When we react with anger to unfair treatment at the time that it occurs and direct it at the person or situation responsible, this is reasonable, justifiable, and healthy and can often better our world.

When love prevails in a family, anger can be expressed without damaging family relationships. A strong love and respect between people can weather angry feelings and can grow from the free expression of them. Contrary to what movies, TV, and magazines may say, no real love relationship can ever be all sweetness and light, all smiles, hugs, and praise. It is downright suspicious when there is a complete absence of frank expressions of anger in a family or in any love relationship. When parents disagree and express anger to one another, children often find this upsetting and threatening to their security. But when they know there is a strong cement of mutual love and respect between their parents, they can look on interparental battles merely as expressions of normal conflict that imperfect human beings have to work out. When children sense that all does not go well between their parents, the expression of anger can terrify them. When there isn't a solid family relationship, for whatever reason, it is more difficult for children to know how and where to express anger; but we can be sure that anger exists, and it is logical that it should.

Even the infant has reason to be angry at times. He has to let his parents know that he needs certain things, and even the wisest of parents does not always know when he needs what. If the infant does not receive the food he desires and feels pains of hunger, he screams with anger. He is frustrated by being hungry, and if the food is postponed for even a longer period of time, his signal of anger flashes even more. (Have you noticed that when you are hungry, you are more prone to feel angry with people?) If this kind of frustration happens often enough to an infant, then another signal turns on inside him—fear. He may become fearful that the people upon whom he depends for his sustenance and survival may let him down again. Anger and fear, fear and anger interact constantly, and it is often difficult to separate them.

Children have the potentialities for growth and development at birth. It is clear that they have needs that must be satisfied in order for them to live. Children want the freedom to be themselves. Children do not want to be encumbered with restrictions, although some controls are reassuring, some boundaries comforting. It is frightening to feel out of control. Children seek some controls, certain standards, and guidance. These enable them to form their own judgments. In a sense, these standards are also an indication to children that their parents care for them. The parents who don't care don't want to be bothered having to control or guide their children. Children, often without realizing it, want and need the word *stop* sometimes to help them to control themselves and also to provide a useful target against which to exercise their energies. Children, by virtue of being children, need to explore, to question, to challenge, to test out, to experiment, even to cross boundaries in order to find out and learn for themselves.

Parents, by virtue of being parents, have the job of preparing children for social living as well as guiding their development as unique persons. It is within the training ground of the family that children are first taught ways to eat, to use a toilet, to wash and to learn various health and safety measures. It is also usual for parents to teach sharing, taking turns, considering the wishes of others, postponing or giving up certain activities for the sake of the group. Parents are carriers of tradition, messengers of society. Parents, by virtue of being parents, are required to set limits. For their own good, as well as for the good of their children, parents have to insist upon a reasonable amount of conformity to their standards, to exercise restraints and controls, to enforce restrictions, to make demands, and to see that their children meet certain obligations. There are some parents who go way beyond a reasonable setting of limits, whose unreasonable demands are guided by their own ambitions and unhappiness. Their children often go way beyond a reasonable protesting against limits and restrictions.

As you can see, there are some opposing pulls even in the most healthy parent-child relationship. There are natural tensions between any two generations. There is normal conflict and there are frustrations between the two generations even when both are being quite reasonable. It is predictable that parents will be angry with their children many times. And they are. It is predictable that children will be angry with their parents many times. And they are.

Do your parents believe it is wrong and sinful for you to be angry? Do they show you by their own actions, as well as by their words, how they feel about anger? Do you feel guilty when you are angry at being treated in an unjust manner? Do you feel that your angry feelings are living proof of your unworthiness as a person or, at the very least, show your immaturity? What do you do when you are angry?

Most of us have been taught that we should not have angry feelings. But if we still have them, most of us are taught that we should not express our anger, because it is impolite and "other people won't like us."

Many of us are taught that love and anger are incompatible. They are not. When anger is a reaction to being hurt, frustrated, or deprived of something and can be openly expressed, it can be dealt with. Then ways can be found to enhance a relationship. Very often, this openness increases the love and understanding between people and deepens their closeness.

When obedience to parents springs only from fear and a sense of duty to parents comes only from guilt, there are angry wounds that linger. When a boy is not allowed to express anger in his family, when he is shamed and punished for feeling angry with his parents, his anger becomes an infection in his system that is easily aggravated by unhealthy conditions in the school, neighborhood, and society. This is the pus that may fester into juvenile delinquency.

If a child grows up learning that he is "bad" for being angry and showing it, every time he feels angry he feels that it is the "badness" exploding inside him. Then every frustrating experience he has reinforces his feelings of inadequacy. This increases his anger. If on top of this, because of the color of the skin he was born with or the religion he adheres to, he is subjected to experience after experience of humiliation and rejection and he tries to bury his angry feelings about these as well as about his parents, is it surprising that all of a sudden these feelings explode into an antisocial action?

Sometimes there are situations in which we must make a real effort to control the expression of our anger. Parents have to teach little children to control and restrain anger to some extent in order to keep them from harming themselves and others. Wise parents reassure the child that they understand why she is angry. On the other hand, the parents cannot permit the child to club everyone who annoys her, pinch her brother for teasing her, throw sand in the eyes of the companion who grabbed her shovel away, or kick the aunt who won't even notice that she exists. When a child feels small and helpless in a big world or feels resentful for a number of reasons, expressing her anger over unfair treatment protects her—and sometimes even gets her the shovel back. Wise parents encourage the child to find more socially acceptable and constructive ways to express these feelings, rather than trying to erase the feelings or pretending they don't exist.

Since a tot wants her parents' love, approval, and praise, usually she tries to please them. This means she gradually gives up the biting, the kicking, the pinching, the spitting, the hitting, and so on that she has used to express her anger and to protect herself. Of course, there are even some adults who are loath to surrender these useful techniques. In some ethnic groups, physical aggression is not looked upon askance as it is in other groups. In some groups, verbal assault is more permissible. Using words as weapons, not only swear words, can replace striking out at others physically. Since we all feel anger, it finds its expression one way or another.

All of us can remember times when we have used swear words, dirty words, curse words to express, among other things, anger. Sometimes we use them just for effect, to make us look big or grown up, but often we spit them out in anger and they relieve us. Words can be used in other ways that are quite devastating. Words can hurt us to the core, notwithstanding the old adage about sticks and stones. It is not uncommon to hear a little child say, "I hate you! You can't be my friend. I won't invite you to my birthday party. You're a baby!" When a child is less direct, even though he is saying the same thing, he says, "Abracadabra, I'll turn you into a snake. I'll make you disappear forever. I'll hide your mommy and daddy in the forest. I'll send the boogeyman to get you if you don't watch out."

As we become more sophisticated, we ridicule and tease more. We can use humor in a vicious, biting manner. When our anger is provoked, often it is expressed by jokes made at the expense of others. This is an effective way to belittle others, although never completely gratifying. We attack others and at the same time protect ourselves with a joke. Have you ever been made fun of, and then when you said your feelings were hurt, the person asked you, "What's the matter—can't you take a joke?" Take a look at the jokes you find the funniest and see whether they touch upon your fears, guilt, or anger.

In authoritarian countries, a prevalent form of revolt at present is the jokes whispered secretly about the dictators and their failures. Jokes pass all around the country about food shortages, government red tape, privileges enjoyed by the leaders, deprivations experienced by the masses, and the twenty-one-gun salute fired at the dictator by mistake. They afford an opportunity for laughter and are a safe outlet for feelings of anger. In our country, out in the open, we spoof our parents, mothers-in-law, policemen, generals, business and labor leaders, and many people in authority, with our President often leading the roster.

Words can be weapons of anger, but they don't always have to be talked. They can be written, and they can be sung. Many folk songs are songs of anger and protest. This may explain part of their wide appeal. In the process of seeking and struggling to gain freedoms and liberty, songs —both old and new—against oppression give us an outlet for angry feelings and a sense of satisfaction. Consider some of the words in "Go Down Moses" or in the song of the Freedom Riders and those against segregation in the South called "We Shall Overcome." There are many more songs that have as targets those people or things that deprive us of a good existence, such as "The Boll Weevil," about the insect that destroyed cotton crops for years. There are a whole host of labor union songs that were songs of great resentment in the days before the labor unions had established their position in society. There are many songs poking fun at the boys and many poking fun at the girls and an abundance of songs about untrue lovers and unhappy relationships. Swear words or harsh phrases can be sung with great gusto. Singing together gives us a sense of support and solidarity and can assuage our fears and our anger.

Playing the piano, beating the drums, blowing the trumpet, and picking the strings of a banjo can be outlets for expressing angry feelings just as singing can. When we don't use words or music, we can use our bodies to express anger.

Sometimes participating in active sports can be a satisfactory way of giving vent to angry feelings. Even being a spectator at football or baseball games, races, rodeos, and wrestling matches can give us a vicarious thrill and an outlet. Bowling, throwing a ball, tennis, even mild old croquet can be handy ways to express anger. Dancing, modern expressive dance as well as various forms of popular dancing, can also be a way to express angry feelings and protest. Modern dance itself was a protest against traditional forms of dance such as ballet and was an outgrowth of the need for free expression of feelings.

Painting or photography as social commentary, cartooning, sculpting, and wood-carving are fields in the vast world of art in which angry feelings can be woven into the fabric of the art world. The theater has had a tradition of staging conflicts. In the rage of a Lear or an Othello, Shakespeare, who was a master psychologist, uncovered the forces that caused such feeling, and he portrayed through drama the self-destruction and harm to others that came as a result. Plays, operas, movies, skits deal frequently with feelings of anger. Playing a part in a skit often affords us the golden opportunity of acting out anger or caricaturing the kind of person we do not like. Have you seen or been in any plays recently in which signals of anger were flashing throughout the scenario?

Instead of taking a long look at the anger we feel at the "no, stop, awful, terrible, worse, worse than ever before, impossible, no, stop!" that we hear all the time from parents, teachers, and society in general, often we find convenient routes of escape.

When there is no anger expressed openly in a family, we can be sure that it is neatly bottled up and stored on a shelf but will not magically disappear from our lives.

*When no anger is expressed in a family, it gets bottled up and
may explode later.*

The anger clings to us, and we nurse it into other experiences. Many of us seek refuge in the "fix," in sweets or other soothing foods, in the long cool drink, in the sensations of sexual relations, in complete lethargy and daydreams, in any activity that can divert us from our anger.

Stored-up anger can be displayed in other ways that are turned inward on ourselves, that make our own lives more uncomfortable. Excessive nail-biting, teeth-grinding, bed-wetting, constant headaches, chronic depression, and being accident-prone can be results of stored-up anger. We can take it out on ourselves by being overly self-critical, overly humble and self-sacrificing, depriving ourselves of opportunities that we might otherwise enjoy. It almost sounds as if we are punishing ourselves sometimes for having angry feelings. We all indulge in some of these things, but when they seem beyond our control, they are excessive.

Self-imposed starvation, alcoholism, drug addiction, unwanted pregnancies, even the practicing of sexual aberrations, as well as the extreme of suicide, are not only ways of punishing ourselves but also ways of getting back at the people we care about, making them suffer. We don't necessarily plan it this way, but inside our able selves, forces are at work bringing this about. Isn't our anger, both free and stored-up, still directed at the people we care about and who count most in our lives?

The seemingly kind, gentle, sweet, mild little man who drives a car like a maniac is releasing his stored-up anger, and his means of release can often harm others as well as himself. The "litter bug" may be littering the streets with stored-up anger as well as with papers. The youngster who starts fires regularly and those who frequently steal objects that may have little value to them are, among other things, releasing some stored-up anger. Calling the fire department when there is no fire, harassing people with silly or frightening telephone calls or poison pen letters, and getting into a fight with anybody who comes along are ways held-back feelings of anger cling to us and affect others.

These clinging feelings of anger can lead us to join extreme groups protesting one thing or another. Sometimes the group we join benefits our neighborhood or country, and sometimes it is against the best interests of our country. Our anger often finds expression as well as support in group protest, group action. If our schoolteachers, coaches, scout leaders, recreation directors have stored-up anger at work inside them, it can release itself in excessive discipline and unreasonable prohibitions and punishment. A certain amount of discipline is necessary with any group, but the person allowed to administer corporal punishment to keep students in line may use it as a weapon of hate. This is the terrible risk we take when we allow corporal punishment. It is clear that stored-up anger within ourselves often gets shoved onto others who are not in the least responsible for our anger.

It takes some lonely probing and some solitary exploration into ourselves to track down some of the hidden feelings of fear and guilt that are involved in our feelings of anger. The person who is indiscriminately angry at the world and, conversely, the person who prides himself on never being angry share the same discomfort of denying their feelings of anger. When we are overcritical of, and overreact to, faults in others, this is the cue to look for the same faults in ourselves, which may even be well hidden from ourselves. When we become excessively impatient and angry at certain traits in our parents and other family mem-

bers, friends, teachers, can it be that we are being unfair
and that we are reacting to those traits we don't like in
ourselves?

If you are always late, does it bother you when someone
else is always late? Does someone else's stinginess drive
you to distraction, whereas your own you call intelligent
frugality? To see in somebody else a messy and dirty appearance annoys some of us to the point of anger. To call
someone else dirty makes ourselves and others conscious of
how clean we are, even though we may fear we are dirty.
Often when we say with deep emotion, "The thing I hate
most is a quitter," deep down inside of us, one of the things
we may feel guilty about or fear is that we may be quitters.
When we refer frequently to people as being "stupid," can
this express some of our fears about ourselves? When we
say we hate the "egghead," or the studious person, could
we be jealous and fearful that he may excel us? Our pet
hates and our pet fears are often interlocked and inter-
twined.

The people most out of tune with their own feelings
tend to be the people who are hardest on the next guy's
feelings.

Your employer belligerently bellows at you when the fuse
burns out.

Your teacher has a bad fall coming to school and unfairly
picks on the students.

Your friend missed the first bus and pushes the old lady in
front of him on the next bus.

Your date furiously and continuously blasts his horn at the
line of cars held up in traffic.

Your salesgirl, just criticized by her boss, heatedly slings a
dress at you.

Your father, having just lost a business deal, finds fault with everything you do.

Your mother, not feeling well, screams at you for talking on the telephone.

You immediately denounce and attack a new boy who has just entered your class.

Your parents told you to come home early, so you act sassy with a bus driver.

You slug your baby brother the afternoon you hear you did not make the team.

You lost a school election, so you slam the door in your mother's face.

Your teacher complains about your grades, so you complain that your father doesn't treat you with respect.

You were not invited to a party, so you don't tip the waitress at the soda fountain.

Someone hurts your feelings, so you hurt the feelings of others who have nothing to do with this situation.

Have you been in any of these situations?

Can you think of times when you were angry with your parents, your sister, your brother, your friend, your date, your teacher and instead of dealing with the person you were angry with, someone else reaped the venom of your bad mood? Perhaps you were treated badly or you treated someone else badly when the situation did not warrant it. Then feelings of stored-up anger were thrust onto the nearest, most convenient person or object. This is "scape-goating." We all do it to one degree or another and have been for a long time. In Leviticus 16:21–22 it says:

And Aaron shall lay both his hands upon the head of the live goat, and confess over him all the iniquities of the children of Israel, and all their transgressions, even all their sins; and he shall put them upon the head of the goat, and shall send him away by the hand of an appointed man into the wilderness. And the goat shall bear upon him all their iniquities . . .

Maybe we each need to have a live goat to let our frustrations out on instead of hurting people and ourselves so much.

Scapegoating runs the gamut from overblaming to the fanatic persecution of people innocent of crime, from kicking a dog to smashing a plate. It involves hurting others, be it by the casual remark, name-calling, teasing, bullying, degradation, or physical attack. Scapegoating attacks our dignity. It makes us feel hurt and threatened and angry. When we cause discomfort and unhappiness to an innocent bystander or cause a man to lose his job or a girl to lose her boyfriend because our stored-up anger needs a target, then it is vital that we take a long look at our angry feelings and examine how we displace them.

The distance between scapegoating and prejudice is not far, and soon our stored-up anger attaches itself to convenient targets in minority groups. Who gets your goat today? Instead of blaming the persons we are annoyed with, it may be socially acceptable in our neighborhood, family group, or country to blame the Negroes, the whites, the Puerto Ricans, the foreigners, the Jews, the Catholics for all our troubles. We not only blame them in conversations, but also engage in or quietly support discriminatory actions. Often we pass on jokes slandering these groups. Prejudice may be related to our economic situation when we feel threatened in our livelihood. It may be related to the political situation in a country when one group fears that another group will take over. For self-perpetuation, the leadership may encourage wholesale prejudice, as Hitler did against the Jews. But prejudice also has to do with how we handle our anger and how we feel about ourselves.

In some of the Asian countries where the Chinese minority consists of wealthy, hard-working businessmen, harsh laws have been enacted and tight restrictions placed upon them when the economic situation in the country has been shaky or when there have been political tensions because the national leadership felt threatened. In South Africa, the political leaders have convinced a majority of the white electorate, without valid evidence, that their lives and fortunes are completely threatened and put in such imminent danger by the black South Africans that they must enact harsh discriminatory laws against them and take away as many rights as possible. The leaders have created fear among the minority white population, and the fear has turned into anger that they should be so threatened. The attitudes supported by unfair prohibitions, unreasonable laws, and violation of human rights have created such fear and hate among the Africans that the most minor incident could set off mass slaughter and violence.

Prejudice and scapegoating are misuses of anger. Anger can be used constructively when directed against the forces that cause it. Take a look at the many countries in Asia, Africa, and around the world where colonialism has kept people submerged and where colonial powers have often made enormous profits by taking unfair advantage of the people and the resources of the country. When we consider the beginnings of our country (the Indians never did get a good deal), we find that the American Revolution came about because the colonists were angry at receiving unfair treatment and being exploited, used, manipulated. Just as the individual person can use his anger to defend himself against wrongful authority, so countries can defend themselves against wrongful authority.

We return to the need for separating out the difference between complete license and responsible freedom. It might be nice to feel free to drive down any side of the street that pleases us, at any speed we desire, in any pattern that satisfies us, but it endangers others, so we have the freedom to drive—with limitations. Laws are usually a useful weapon for defending the majority in a democracy. We have to surrender the pleasurable feelings of license for the common good, just as we need the freedom to rebel against unjustified authority for the common good.

If, for example, we are given a speeding ticket by a police officer when we know for sure we have not exceeded the speed limit, this is definitely an injustice. It is quite normal for us to feel angry in this situation and to try to do something about it. Since our anger is justified and appropriate to the situation, there is no reason for us to feel guilty. It takes time, effort, and guts to go to the police station and complain about the unjust treatment, but many have done just that and have not had to pay the fine. Teachers who have been cruel and harmful have been dismissed from their jobs because students channeled their anger to the proper authorities, and investigation and action followed. Can you think of other situations where your anger or the anger of a group you knew brought about positive change in a situation?

We all know that it is not possible to act effectively every time we feel anger. Why is it that often we do not direct our anger against the true sources of our frustration? Some possible reasons:

fear of punishment
fear of losing love and approval of people we depend on
fear of losing friends or not being liked by a group
fear of endangering already shaky relations
fear of loss of prestige or position in the community
fear of loss of a job
the inaccessibility of the person who angered us
not being aware that we are angry
being aware that we are angry but not being sure at whom

Sometimes, even when we are sure we cannot win an argument or change a situation, we still express our anger directly at those who frustrate us. The little boy who knows his big brother can beat him up will often still fight the older boy for being unfair to him, perhaps desperately hoping that one day he will be strong enough to silence his tormentor. By the same token, perhaps the Hungarian revolt in 1956 and certainly the East German uprisings in 1953 were expressions of deep anger from people who were willing to risk their lives knowing they could not win but gambling on the infinitesimal chance that they might.

Anger is too much a part of our lives to be denied. We need to tune in to our anger signals, relieve the pressures if we can, and communicate as directly as possible with the sources of difficulty. When the shrill forces of anger are excessive, how about taking some time to investigate our inner equipment and attempting to track down the real sources of trouble? The more we can use the invaluable tool of insight to probe into ourselves, the more we can better our lives.

5. Guilt and Guilty Feelings

GUILT IS PART of the emotional legacy of man. It goes way back to the beginning of a peopled world, when families began. The family began with a relationship between two persons, each different and separate, unlike any other. In order to survive, they had to work out a life together, cooperate, share, work out conflicts. They had to adhere to certain standards or fall heir to guilt. Their children grew up learning these standards, and parents as well as children were judged guilty when they defied these standards and felt guilty when they thought of defying them.

Soon there were more families. Because of the dangers of existence, family units were quick to realize that they needed other family units for protection, support, and help. It was then that communities developed and grew. Communities could not exist without certain standards and rules of behavior. Any large group needs a common framework of discipline to keep it together. Within this framework, be it for a large group or a community, each person needs to be allowed a certain degree of personal flexibility and individuality. But for the community itself to survive, its members have to live by its rules. In the beginning days of the world, if members of the community lived by its rules they were rewarded with approval, acceptance, and security. If they did not, they suffered some form of punishment. The rules, which are also standards, principles, values, codes of behavior, devised in a particular community became the essence of "good" behavior as opposed to "bad," "right" as opposed to "wrong." The standards devised in one community were not necessarily the same as those established in another community. The location of the community, the heat or cold of the climate, the physical attributes of the region, whether hunting or fishing or agriculture was the means of livelihood—all influenced the rules that the people in that community created for themselves. There were many differences but essential similarities in all communities. No community yet has ruled that "thou shalt hate thy father and thy mother."

The rules and standards that are an integral part of group living are taught to each of us from infancy on through our lives by our parents, religious groups, friends, communities, schools, cities, states, and nation. We learn these by example, admonition, law, and study. If we act against the accepted rules and standards of our parents and/or our community, we are judged guilty. If we wish we could break the rules, if we think we may have broken the rules, if we almost break the rules, if we contemplate breaking the rules, then we may feel guilty.

To *be* guilty we must commit an act or deed. Some of us acknowledge our guilt. Some of us feel innocent when we are guilty of an act. Some of us feel guilty for *not* committing an act. To *feel* guilty can be our response to almost anything and everything. Is there anyone who has not had both experiences? While we may feel guilty about almost anything and everything, depending upon the kind of person we are and the experiences we have had, often we do not recognize guilt feelings for what they are. The more un-pleasant the feelings (and guilt feelings are downright un-comfortable), the more likely we are to bury the feelings and try to "forget" them. Although our attempts to forget are often highly successful, the guilty feelings do not dis-appear as we wish they would. The guilt feelings that lurk clandestinely inside us are our own worst enemies, for these marauders can cripple our relationships, paralyze our ac-tions, and deform the love between people. Guilt feelings isolate us from others. They can make us overreact, overdo, and underenjoy. Guilt feelings can make us unnecessarily hard on ourselves.

The more our guilty feelings lurk unrecognized within us, the more they consume us and govern our actions.

Not all guilty feelings are necessarily bad. As a matter of fact, something is the matter if we don't have any. Feelings of guilt can, to some extent, be utilized constructively for society and can serve as a safeguard for all of us. Imagine the mess we would be in if we did not feel guilty about killing others! That would be a rather drastic solution to the world's problem of population explosion. If most of us did not feel guilty about stealing, lying, cheating, com-mitting adultery, there would be chaos. Do you think if we had more guilt feelings we might prevent war? Or do our host of guilt feelings sometimes result in war? Perhaps some wars and battles have been avoided by guilt feelings. Would there be even more suffering in the world than there is already if we did not have guilt feelings about not help-ing people in need?

What causes us to feel guilty? How intense are these feel-ings? What do we do? These questions are what we need to explore in order to tune into our warning signals, our guilty feelings.

Guilt feelings are inevitable
because we have parents who have standards (some that promote growth and some that don't)
because we and our parents live in a society that has standards (some for the common good and some not necessarily so)
because we as children come to know these standards (some we respect and some we don't)
because we as children come to accept these standards automatically (some we know about and some we don't).

We might not, cannot, could not, should not, will not adhere to these standards all the time, so we feel guilty!

We often start feeling guilty from the time we have the first independent thought and engage in our first independent act, probably before we are even one year old. We continue to experience guilt feelings to one degree or another until the day we die. We all feel guilty about certain things, but no two people ever react in exactly the same way. When several of us are placed in the same awkward situation, some of us will feel guilty and some of us will not. Some of us will know when we are feeling guilty, some of us won't know, some of us will not want to know. And none of us, even the most enlightened among us, will know every single time we feel guilty.

Guilt feelings are uncomfortable, sometimes painful, certainly annoying and difficult to deal with. They work inside us even when no one is watching us and when everything around us is quiet and serene. Guilt feelings that suddenly rise within us may have nothing to do with the present situation we are in. They can be very subtle and elusive, just as they can blare within us in a situation in which it is abundantly clear why they have arisen.

Often our guilt feelings signal that our parents and other people whom we care about, and who are influential in our lives, would disapprove of what we are doing or not doing, saying or not saying, of what we are thinking, wanting, desiring. We are being warned to apply the inner brakes and control what we are doing or be prepared to suffer the consequences. We are being urged to stop short, think, fulfill obligations, take actions, or do nothing.

Guilt feelings are indispensable to the development of our conscience, and it is our conscience that makes us feel guilty. Almost everyone develops a conscience, whether we listen to it or not. The old maxim, "Let your conscience be your guide," is usually part of our upbringing. Our conscience is primarily modeled on our parents. Could it be the secret agent of our parents working inside us? Our conscience is our internal guidebook to behavior. It is the gentle or harsh parent within us indicating what is acceptable, or unacceptable, good or bad, right or wrong, just or unjust, true or false, that which helps us and that which hinders us.

None of us is born with a conscience. We are born equipped with senses that indicate to us that which feels good and that which doesn't feel good. That which is painful and threatening to a small child, he labels bad. That which is pleasing and comforting, he labels good. But these responses do not constitute a conscience at work.

A child loves those who love him, and he usually wants to be like those he loves. When he does not feel loved, he may try all the more to please those around him to gain acceptance. His conscience develops from his need for approval and acceptance, from the rewards and punishments he receives, and from his desire to model himself on the people he admires. In order to develop a properly functioning conscience, the little child must give up some pleasures, just as earliest man had to give up some pleasures for the welfare of his community, for the utlimate good. In order to give up purposefully one thing for another, we must control our urges, desires, pleasures. (What a nuisance!) We must consider more than the immediate, the "now," and instead think about the future, the "later." This means that we cannot focus only on ourselves but have to widen our lenses to include others. It means we have to visualize three important words in our vocabulary—*in order to*.

You must give up hitting *in order to* be liked by others.
You must not eat now *in order to* eat with the family later.
You must go to sleep now *in order to* get up early tomorrow.
You must study now *in order to* profit from school.

Part of a parent's difficult job is to require that as a child grows, he must restrict, inhibit, even oppose many of his own immediate urges and impulses in order to meet certain standards and enhance his own development. Control and restraint are not inherited but learned through the actions, the teachings, and, above all, through the love from and the love of others.

To begin with, an infant has only limited muscular control, and since his nervous system is not fully developed, he is limited in controlling himself. The toddler is encouraged to and often will try to control himself, sometimes for the reward of a kiss, a smile, a loving pat, praise, and recognition. His parents' approval and disapproval are the outside controls exerted on his behavior. This starts him on the development of his own controls.

In our first two years, we grow faster and develop more, proportionately, than at any other time in our lives. Two-year-olds are preoccupied with walking, running, climbing, jumping, talking, singing, eating by themselves, using the toilet, mastering a multitude of manual and intellectual skills that older children take for granted. Two-year-olds are talented discoverers, scientists, and adventurers, busy exploring and testing out the exciting world around them that each day provides something new. In the midst of experimenting, a two-year-old may feel like decorating the living room with his mother's lipstick. He may anticipate that his mother will be angry, because she was angry the last time he did something like that. He might even feel a slight twinge of guilt as a result of her anger. But he does not look upon his act as a moral or ethical issue involving the destruction of property, causing extra work, and therefore an unjust act. Why? Because he has no conscience yet. He has no internal standards that govern his behavior. He has only fear of disapproval, fear of withdrawal of love, fear of punishment and reprisal.

Slowly, when he is ready for school, some automatic stop signs start to work inside him. Within the older child, well along in school, a reliable conscience starts to take over. The gentle or harsh parent within the older child curbs excessive will. It inhibits some spontaneity and independence in order to control his behavior, in order to aid his development and protect society. To make him obedient and easier to master or deal with is only part of it. When he develops a conscience, he develops a dependence upon himself that can make him dependable, hopefully enabling him to better his own interests and those of others.

Guilt feelings can activate our conscience.

Guilt feelings can prevent repetition of unworthy or harmful acts.

Guilt feelings can encourage useful acts that benefit people.

Guilt feelings can under- or overactivate our conscience.

Guilt feelings can put the whole personality under arrest by overaccusing, overthreatening, overpunishing.

Guilt feelings can promote harmful acts.

A good and effective conscience behaves like a good and effective parent. When you were very little, you felt unhappy almost every time you disobeyed your parents. You knew that you displeased them, and perhaps you feared that they would not love you so much or that they might abandon you. You probably felt guilty every time you had what you considered to be a nasty thought about them or whenever you impetuously or in a moment of anger wished them some kind of ill. Unless you had parents who made the clear distinction between the things you did and the person you were, you were likely to feel not only that what you did or thought was bad but that you were a very bad person. Your family's camera view of you printed a picture of yourself in your own mind. If your family indicated one way or another that you were not a good person, then the picture you framed of yourself was pretty ugly. Chances are that as you grew up, you continued to feel ugly and worthless every time you felt guilty. Now when you feel guilty about something, how do you react? Can you separate out your feelings of guilt from your picture of yourself? Or do you read the guilt signal not as a warning but as confirmation of your own utter worthlessness? Does it vary with the circumstances?

We come back to the eternal process of giving up something for something else, giving up a certain amount of comfort and ease for greater fulfillment as a person. If we don't try to achieve independence from our parents, it is likely that we will feel guilty and resentful. In attempting to achieve independence, it is to be expected that there is conflict. Guilt feelings breed quickly in conflict and frequently arise as an offshoot of love. Guilt feelings are safeguards so long as they do not destroy the love or need for love from which they spring. If we love someone, we feel guilty if we suspect that we have hurt them.

Parents satisfied within their own lives can usually help their children become self-reliant and permit them to make their own mistakes. Such parents (as all parents must) will still disagree with, criticize, scold, and sometimes shame and punish their children. They will feel free to say "no" and "don't," but will not reject the child along with the child's behavior. Thus a manageable degree of guilt floats back and forth in these parent-child relationships.

The way our parents handle their feelings and the way our parents react to our feelings will influence how much our guilt feelings affect our lives. For example, if a little girl hurls a building block at her brother in a fit of anger, it is appropriate for her to feel somewhat guilty for that act. Even if she had good cause to be angry with him, how she dealt with her anger could have caused great injury or harm. If her parents accept her feelings of anger but declare that she handled them badly, they may help her find other ways to express angry feelings. She needs their help in learning control. When she is little, her parents *are* her conscience, and if they help her rather than condemn her, her guilt feelings will not overwhelm her.

But if this same girl is severely punished or shamed and

made to feel that she, rather than her angry action, is "bad," she is placed in a cell of her own feelings of worthlessness. She feels guilty for having had angry feelings. The angry feelings plunge down deeper and increase in intensity. All her fears of being punished and being excluded from the family go underground. These feelings accumulate and smolder under a heavy layer of guilty feelings. Although undetected, these feelings seek and find expression in unsuspected ways. They do not disappear into thin air. If this kind of experience happens often enough to this girl, she may act out her feelings in bizarre ways, such as washing perpetually, symbolically cleaning off her guilt. (Remember Lady Macbeth?) She may go to the extreme of never being able to touch another person comfortably. She may go to the extreme of never allowing herself to throw a ball or play any active game. Without knowing it, she may fear a loss of all self-control. She may fear that these mildly aggressive acts will serve to explode the guilt, fear, and anger smoldering inside her. These are not farfetched reactions. They happen frequently. But, luckily, most of us do not go to these extremes.

The unrecognized and consuming feelings of guilt that mix in the same underground soil with fear and anger plant effectively within us that devastating feeling of being "no good."

Our glib talk about inferiority complexes, superiority complexes, and lack of self-confidence is our way of describing what is essentially that devastating feeling of being "no good."

What words skyrocket into your mind when you hear the

word *guilt? Anger, fear, hate, blame, shame, humiliation, crime, sin, evil, morals, rules, laws, justice, truth, responsibility, duty, obligation?*

It is no wonder that feelings of guilt have so much influence on our lives, our relationships, our actions, the history pages of tomorrow! Look at some of the expressions we use to identify guilt and add some of your own:

> Look me straight in the eye.
> I can see the guilt written all over your face.
> You have the guilty look.
> It is obvious that she is plagued by guilt.
> You could see the guilt sticking out all over him.

We also make many comparisons using the word *guilty,* such as:

> Guilty as hell
> Guilty as sin
> Guilty as a hound-dog
> Guilty as a jay bird
> Guilty as the devil
> Guilty as all get-out

We are quick to point the finger at someone. We are often only too ready to accuse, to blame, to shame someone else. Why? Usually, those people who feel the most guilty inside themselves do the most blaming and shaming outside themselves. Blaming and shaming are social tools we use to defend and protect ourselves. Blaming and shaming make other people feel guilty. These tools are most often used as a last resort in getting others to do what we want them to do. They are used constantly in scapegoating when our own fears, anger, and guilt feelings force us to point a finger at someone else. Blaming belittles, humiliates, often hurts another person. Shaming implies publicly displaying a person's inadequacies or mocking him. We "bury" our faces in shame, "hang" our heads in shame, and often wish we could disappear off the face of the earth.

"Shame on you! You don't want your friends to think you are a baby," says a mother to her teen-age daughter in front of her daughter's friends. The girl has not done what the mother wanted, so the mother uses this means to control her. This degrading, humiliating act is designed to work on the girl's guilt feelings, but instead it may increase her anger, which may cause mother and daughter more trouble in the long run.

The schoolteacher who, in front of the whole class, shames and ridicules the one student who has failed to bring in her homework may succeed in receiving the student's homework on time from then on, but at what personal cost to the student? To convince a person of her own wickedness may make her obedient—or just the reverse. The youngster who throws ink at someone might well feel some guilt about it, but does he have to be made to feel like a murderer? Do you sometimes blame and shame your sisters and brothers just to make yourself feel good and righteous and superior? Do you shame your friends into doing what you want them to do at times? If you are baby-sitting and feel unsure of your ability to control the children in your charge, do you resort to shaming and teasing them? Most of us tend to use the tool or weapon of shame when we feel unsure of ourselves.

Societies, old and new, have used public shaming as a means of punishing and isolating members in order to exact group conformity to the accepted rules. It was common practice in the days of the Puritans to put the scarlet *A* on the adultress and to place a man in the stocks for non-payment of debts.

Mahatma Gandhi, one of the great leaders of India and founder of the nonviolent passive-resistance movement, decided to use the social tool of shame to stimulate guilt feelings in the British in order to speed up the granting of independence to his nation. He found that shaming through use of nonviolent parades, sit-ins, fasts, and the like planted the guilt feelings that in turn activated the consciences of many of the British. He discovered also that shaming demonstrated clearly to Indians and British alike that they must commit themselves to something and work either for or against the independence movement. Many people believe that shaming was the weapon that hastened the independence of India.

American Negroes, in their fight for constitutional rights, are shaming America right now with their protest marches, sit-ins, Freedom Rides, songs of freedom, and other mechanisms of nonviolent action. When others are violent to them, they do not strike back. They are utilizing the weapon of shame to stir up guilt feelings of other Americans about prejudice and discrimination.

Every minority problem is a symptom of a majority problem. When the majority feels insecure economically, socially, or emotionally, it turns against the minority. But the guilt feelings of members of the majority may become so uncomfortable that they are forced to reduce oppression. After a truce had been worked out in Birmingham, Alabama, the followers of Dr. Martin Luther King were satisfied that Birmingham had reached an accord with its conscience.

Guilt feelings can activate consciences. On the other

hand, guilt feelings can be shoved aside along with consciences. When guilt feelings and consciences are shoved aside, they are usually replaced by an outside authority that determines the good and the bad. The Nazis who worked in the concentration camps and gassed millions of Jews were apparently able to shove guilt and conscience aside in the name of doing good for Hitler and Germany. The southerners who have used electric rods and hungry dogs on fellow Americans who happened to be born with darker skins presumably feel no guilt, although suppressed and unacknowledged guilt may have caused some of this violence.

Normally, we feel guilty when we harm someone else. We feel guilty when we deprive people of things that are rightfully theirs. Normally, we expect to have guilt feelings when we break a law, destroy someone else's property, take something that doesn't belong to us, lie, cheat, rape, or murder. Our laws and standards of behavior state that these are reprehensible acts, and if we commit them we are guilty.

But what kinds of things make us *feel* guilty? Could these be some of the many thoughts, actions, reactions that make us feel guilty? Do we feel guilty about:

not obeying our parents	or	obeying our parents
rejecting our parents' standards	or	accepting our parents' standards
rejecting our friends' standards	or	accepting our friends' standards
having friends our parents don't like	or	not having friends
following others, wanting to follow	or	leading others, wanting to lead
pretending to be what we are not	or	being very much ourselves

hiding genuine feelings	or	sharing feelings
wanting clear-cut rules	or	not wanting any rules
making decisions	or	not being able to make decisions
taking a position, committing ourselves	or	not standing up for what we believe
controlling ourselves too much	or	not being able to control ourselves
criticizing others or gossiping	or	keeping everything to ourselves
asserting ourselves to be noticed	or	staying in the background
getting away with things	or	not trying to get away with things
not liking everyone who likes us	or	falling for flattery
not reciprocating invitations	or	spending time with people we don't like
using an excuse to see someone we like	or	not making an effort
not studying hard enough	or	studying very hard
doing better than others	or	not doing as well as others
being close with friends of the same sex	or	not being interested in the same sex
being underdeveloped	or	being overdeveloped
liking to be touched	or	not liking to be touched
being promiscuous	or	not indulging in any physical relations
desiring physical contact	or	not desiring physical contact
being	or	not being
having	or	not having
wanting	or	not wanting
craving	or	not craving
feeling	or	not feeling

Many of our guilt feelings revolve around our relations with our parents. We are often caught between feeling guilty about not pleasing our parents and feeling guilty about not pleasing our friends. We often pick our friends because they have different standards from our parents. We feel the need for approval from both our friends and our parents. This is a conflict. Often, we heed our friends more than we heed our parents as we grow older. We feel guilty about disobeying our parents, just as Adam and Eve presumably felt guilty about disobeying God. Eve apparently picked the forbidden apple. Adam apparently ate it. The Bible says God banished them from the Garden of Eden as punishment. Is it possible that this punishment not only deprived them of something they wanted but also gave them a chance to assume more personal responsibility, to develop their consciences, and to become more self-reliant? When we disobey, criticize, argue with our parents, we feel guilty not only about disturbing our relationship with them, but also about not showing proper respect for elders as our society may deem we should. Then, too, many religions teach us to "honor" our fathers and mothers. Granted, this is not always easy.

Almost all religions emphasize the preservation of the family unit and the avoidance of the perverse or anything that will harm human life. Most religions postulate a Supreme Being, an all-powerful God, to help us to help ourselves. Within each religion there are rules for living, codes, standards, principles to support us and give us added will power and strength. When we go against these precepts, we feel guilty. The strictness of our religious observance determines the amount of guilt we feel in defying our religious beliefs and can stimulate a lot of feelings of fear and guilt.

All religions are designed to encourage "morality," which means conformity to the accepted standards of virtue. When you hear the word *morality,* does the word *sex* ring in your ears? Most of us associate the word *moral* with the word *sex*, but sex is only one aspect of morality or immorality, just as sex is only one aspect of marriage. Moral or ethical behavior is primarily that which is loving, just, and kind. There are different interpretations of ethics and morality in different parts of the world. It is good and moral to hunt heads in some places and dreadful in other places. It is good and ethical in some places never to kill animals, even flies, and it is unheard of not to in many other places. Do you know what moral code you live by or try to live by? Do you share the same principles of what constitutes "good" and "bad" as your parents? Do you differ with them on some principles? If tomorrow you suddenly became a parent, what would you most want to pass on to your child about standards of behavior?

We learn morality from our parents. It is reinforced or modified by our religion, our community, our friends, and the laws of our state and country. We learn morality not by words alone but by how our parents and others that influence us live their lives. Parental revulsion against the murder of a man, parental indignation at a member of a minority group being excluded from their neighborhood, parental protest against the ganging up of a crowd on one man, and parental honesty in a situation in which it would be easier to lie are our most eloquent lessons in morality.

Most people in most countries preach speaking the truth as a basic lesson in morality. Most of us spend our lives seeking "truth." What is it? If your parents ask you to tell someone they are not home when they are, what does that mean to you? What do you demonstrate to your younger brother and sister when they hear you tell one friend one thing and another friend an entirely different

We feel guilty about the changes that take place in our bodies.

version of the same thing? What did it mean to the young people in Denver, Colorado, who were brought up not to cheat, to find out that their police department had been cheating the public, had admitted to robberies and holdups? Have you ever heard a man you admire tell about the business deal he pulled at the expense of someone else or about the job he may have taken from someone else? Does that not conflict with "love thy neighbor"? Have you ever had a teacher who lectures on democratic ideals and is a tyrant in the classroom? Have you seen detective dramas that preach justice yet imply that what is wrong is that the criminal got caught? These are indications of human frailty, and since none of us is perfect, we often contradict the very principles, ideals, and standards we profess. Our society is particularly talented at this, which can be very demoralizing to us, and confusing.

Our families are our picture window to the world, our beginning view of the world. They lay the basis for later outlooks, attitudes, opinions, values, ethics, morality on which we expand or build or perhaps partially reject. When we feel in conflict with the morality of our family, we feel guilty. When there is conflicting morality between our family and the community, we feel guilty. A consistent code of ethics and morality reduces the guilt feelings we have, but that is an ideal few of us are ever able to achieve. How consistently do we alert a waitress to the fact that she made a mistake on the bill in our favor? Do we always return objects or money that we find? If the brightest guy in the class is sitting next to you and you see his paper, do you copy from him on a test? If you peek at someone else's mail or look through a parent's, a teacher's, a doctor's desk to see what they have written about you or others you know, do you feel guilty? Do your guilt feelings deter you from repeating these acts? Do you speak out all the time when you believe someone is being treated unjustly or hurt unnecessarily?

We in America have always prided ourselves on the liberty and freedom we provide. Yet many Americans bought and sold slaves, created laws against Asians entering our country, and victimized neurotic women who were called "witches." Despite these and many other infractions of our democratic principles, basically we still have more liberty and freedom in America than anywhere else in the world. Some of us feel guilty about the injustices and inequalities in our country. There is a guilt we feel when we do something wrong and a guilt we feel when we do something which most others consider right but which is against our own basic code of behavior. There is a guilt we feel from inactivity. Those of us who may live in all-white neighborhoods may feel guilty about not acting upon our beliefs that any person may live in any neighborhood regardless of race, creed, color. Joining a club or fraternity that excludes others who should belong may produce guilt feelings inside us. Even though we are not doing anything obviously very wrong, we may be going against our conscience, and that makes us feel guilty.

If a law says we should not segregate children in education and we go against that law, we are guilty. Those people who have substituted for their consciences and guilt feelings an outside authority like a Black Muslim or Ku Klux Klan code will go against the law but not against that which they call their conscience or code. Laws were essentially created for the common good and to support the national purpose. Democracy flourishes when law is a product of the collective will. Perhaps democracy counts on our guilt feelings to urge us to respect each person as an individual and to respect our laws.

There is so much that we feel guilty about in the process of growing up that it is a wonder that most of us do grow up and that most of us can enjoy life. We feel uncomfortable, ashamed, guilty about the physical, hormonal changes that take place within our bodies. Our shapes, facial features, voices change. Girls begin to menstruate. Boys begin to shave. Hair develops not only on boys' faces but under armpits and in the pubic regions of both boys and girls. Because of all these changes, we become more aware of our bodies than ever before. We begin to feel strange new impulses, urges, drives, desires that involve our bodies. We feel sensations we have never experienced before. We are curious about these and often very worried about them.

Since the early days of our toilet training, many of us have been brought up to ignore or deny our bodies and bodily sensations. Everything remotely sexual spells danger to some parents. They probably had parents who treated their excretion with disgust and felt rigidly uncomfortable with all sexual sensations. To be aware of, and to show interest in, these new sensations when we have been taught to ignore them makes us feel guilty. To dare to find some of these sensations pleasurable when we have been taught to deny them also makes us feel guilty.

There are other parents who were so rigidly brought up by their parents that they go to the other extreme with their children in the hope that their children will not have sexual inhibitions. Many of these parents parade nude in front of their children and encourage sensations of sexuality. With this attitude, they often defeat their own good intentions, for it is not unusual that their children become preoccupied by all this free-floating sexuality, develop conflicts about being aroused, and ultimately do have guilty feelings. Both extremes of parental attitudes, the very strict and the very permissive, can be equally disturbing to children.

Most of us have grown up hearing the following kinds of myths, to which you can no doubt add many of your own:

If you suck your thumb, it will fall off.
If you play with matches, you will wet your pants.
If you masturbate, you will lose your penis.
If you masturbate, you will go insane.
If you kiss boys, you can become pregnant.

We can assume that these myths were created to frighten us away from these activities, and if we indulge in any of them we are guaranteed to feel guilty. When we discover that these are myths, we tend to feel angry with the people who frightened us with them. Many adults who pass on these myths learned them from their parents, believed them, and never learned anything better. Other adults know they are untrue but find it convenient to use them.

Many parents feel uneasy about most matters of sex, and many parents feel particularly uneasy about masturbation. Their religions may even prohibit willful masturbation. Therefore, parents often shame little children for touching or fondling their genitals. Masturbation does seem to occur in varying degrees at different times in most people's lives, and they feel guilty about it. Children feel guilty even if parents accept masturbation as a harmless act unless practiced to excess, because children learn from others that this is done in private, if at all. We tend to feel awfully guilty about any activities done in private or secretly.

Even though it is common for most boys to experience nocturnal emissions (wet dreams), some boys feel guilty about them. Perhaps nobody prepared them for this eventuality. Even if prepared, boys may feel guilty that wet dreams occur in private and that there is evidence for someone to see. They may feel that the changes going on in their bodies are unclean. Girls who are not prepared for menstruation may feel terrified by it and sometimes too ashamed to ask anyone about it. They may feel guilty and believe that menstruation is unclean and has occurred to punish them. Frequently, we feel guilty about our most normal necessary functions.

The girl who feels that she is overdeveloped, or whose breasts have developed before those of her friends, will wonder whether this is what is supposed to happen. She will sometimes fear she will not be attractive and develops a sense of guilt about how she looks. The girl who develops late or is flat-chested may fear that she is not going to be completely feminine, and guilt creeps into her feeling about her body. Beautiful fashion models are often flat-chested, but on the other hand, the Jayne Mansfield type of figure is supposed to be very sexy. But most girls are self-conscious about their figures. Fears and guilty feelings are based on the attitudes girls sense in their parents, friends, and the country in general.

Boys, just as much as girls, compare the sizes of their parts and their stages of development. If a boy fears his penis is small, he may fear that his masculinity is endangered, and these fears can make him feel most uncomfortable and guilty. If his penis is bigger than most other boys', he may fear abnormality or trouble in sexual relations, and he too may have some feelings of guilt about his physical development. There is a wide range of normal development. Real femininity or true masculinity has little to do with how quickly we develop or the size of our sex organs.

Although most us rather like ourselves, we still have feelings of inadequacy. When we question our very maleness or femaleness, we experience a devastating feeling of inadequacy. It is not unusual for both boys and girls who have close friends of the same sex to worry about whether there is any homosexual element in these relationships and to feel guilty about the possibility. Boys often feel guilty if they don't feel they look 100 per cent masculine as depicted in the movies or on TV—tall, rough, tough, with muscles popping out, hair on the chest, a stubby beard, and a swaggering walk. At the same time, boys often feel guilty for not being quiet enough, gentle enough, polite enough, obedient enough. Why are there such contradictions? What do fathers want of their boys in terms of maleness? What are the images projected for boys on the screen, in books, comic books, in ads?

Parents and society in general encourage boys in athletic activity and aggressiveness. Yet at school, activity and aggressiveness often get them into trouble. Our education is primarily geared to girls, who find it easier to sit still, be neat, polite, and cooperative. Since most teachers are women and many fathers are not at home very much, a boy's identification with maleness is made more difficult. Conflicting standards about what constitutes masculinity (toughness, activity, aggressivness or politeness, cooperativeness, neatness) cause conflict, and guilty feelings follow on the heels of conflict.

In different parts of our country, within different groups in a community, there are different social patterns of dating. On the whole, girls today start dating at an early age, and often a girl feels guilty if she is not particularly interested in boys. You would be surprised at the number of girls under sixteen years of age who are really not interested in boys and in dating. But they start dating and their parents encourage it because popularity is considered a mark of success and girls want recognition from their friends. The parents who push their twelve-year-old girl into dating are usually parents who complain when the same girl indulges in heavy petting at age fourteen. Is this surprising when dating starts so early?

Promiscuity is usually related to a girl's fears and guilt feelings about herself. Indulging in frequent sexual relations can be her attempt to gain reassurance, love, and approval when she feels unsure and perhaps unloved. Sometimes the boys and girls who talk big about their sexual exploits are the ones who are most worried about their sexual prowess. Sometimes they have had no experience or have had unsatisfactory experiences and therefore talk big because they feel so inadequate and so guilty.

In some countries premarital sexual experiences are acceptable. In our country, for the most part, they are not. In our country, most of us have been brought up to believe that having intercourse before marriage is an immoral act. When we know we are going against the standards of our group, we are bound to feel some guilt. Girls feel particular guilt, for they are usually expected to remain virgins, whereas there is a different standard for boys. Boys are encouraged to be virile, practiced, and experienced, yet they are censored for going to houses of prostitution and for the increasing number of teen-age pregnancies. Boys who have sexual relations with prostitutes usually feel guilty because they have realistic fears of catching venereal diseases, because they have to pay money to relieve sexual tensions, and because there is no feeling of love involved. Other boys feel relieved from their guilt by paying the money and treating the whole experience as they would a shopping trip to a department store. But when love is not a part of the picture, sex is primarily struggle, conquest, purely physical relief, and it is usually looked upon as something quite ugly. Guilt feelings are then inevitable.

When a boy and girl experiment with intercourse to find out what it is like, they are usually left with disappointment as well as feelings of guilt. Is it not likely for a boy and girl to feel some guilt when hurried sexual relations take place surreptitiously in the back of a car, under a bush, or on a living-room couch, with parents sleeping down the hall and the couple looking around all the time to make sure that they are not discovered? It is all too frequent that couples who guiltily experimented are suddenly faced with unwanted parenthood.

Boys sometimes tease girls, play on their fears of being frigid or "chicken," or try to make them feel guilty for not playing it "square." Many a girl is told that she will be a dried-up old maid in order to frighten her into submitting to sexual relations. The girls whose fears lead them into submitting to this ruse are usually overcome with guilt feelings afterward. Girls, even more than boys, want sexual relations in the context of a loving relationship, because they want security in the form of a lasting union. Some girls have intercourse in hopes of achieving that lasting relationship, but it rarely works out that the boys marry them.

Girls who do not have intercourse before marriage sometimes feel guilty because they fear that there may be something wrong with them, that they may never get married, or that they are isolating themselves from their crowd of friends and boy friends. Even if a girl sleeps with the man she will marry, she often experiences guilt because she has transgressed the moral code, the conscience, the ethics of most groups in our country. Fear of pregnancy, fear of venereal disease, fear of how premarital sexual experience will affect her marriage are all part of what she experiences. She often feels "impure" or "unclean" because she feels that the sexual act is something impure or unclean.

Can it be that when we talk of the sexual act as being something disgusting, we are talking about it as something separate from an act of deep love between two people? Mind you, television and movies tend to give us false pictures of love, courtship, and marriage and mislead us into dividing sex from love. Their emphasis is not on a mature, loving, cooperative act with two persons each helping the other to the maximum stimulation and pleasure. Their emphasis is not on the mutual concern, the deep sharing and intimacy, the solidarity and oneness of two people in love with each other. Do we understand that there is in deep love the need to control impulses, to postpone satisfactions, to be alert to and respect the needs of each other, to take pleasure in pleasing another person? Unfortunately, even when married, some couples do not realize this or experience this. Usually these couples have guilt feelings about the sexual act and any pleasure associated with it. The same people may treat parenthood as something wonderful, yet reject the process of procreation.

To the guilt-ridden mind, enjoyment of life is often impossible and undesirable and pleasure is sure to bring on punishment. The person driven by guilt can never dare to be satisfied and usually cannot let others be satisfied.

There are parents whose expectations for their children are so high that the children can never come up to their expectations, so the parents will never be satisfied.

Parents who are never satisfied with their children usually are never satisfied with themselves. Usually these are the same parents who feel that their children owe them love and respect, have the duty to obey them and show them gratitude. "Look at what I have sacrificed for you," they say when the child is not obeying. This may make the child feel guilty for having been born. It is a subtle way of punishing a child. Some parents say they sacrificed their health, others stay they sacrificed their careers, others say they sacrificed good times just for their children. Whether or not this is true, guilty feelings flow back and forth between parents and child.

Sacrifice can be a sin offering. The feelings of guilt propel some people into making personal, religious, and economic sacrifices. They may punish themselves by sacrificing something very dear to them, or they may deprive themselves of pleasures they want. Many people feel better after they have sacrificed something, given up something, and for them it is the only way to relieve guilt feelings. There are some people who feel guilt is the mainspring of religious interest. Many religions provide means for the release and relief of guilt feelings through confession of sin or through service to others.

Philanthropy, giving to charity, being a "lady bountiful," and volunteering services are all worthy and necessary activities. They may be stimulated by concern for others and/or guilt feelings. Look at our Peace Corps, which exemplifies a rich nation giving to younger, less-developed nations. There is great good accomplished for people in need of help, and the Peace Corps provides a valuable training ground for our young people. But could we not say that there is an element of guilt involved in the development of the Peace Corps? Could we not suppose that the "haves" feel a little guilty that there are so many "have nots"?

Sometimes the guilt felt by many people and leaders in a country can stimulate many worthwhile activities. Sweden, a completely neutral European country in World War II, cooperated with both the Allies and the Nazis and made much profit, especially in its coal and steel industries. It is said that this made many of its people and leaders feel guilty. Is there a relationship between Sweden's wartime profits and the fact that Sweden has turned out so many "soldiers of peace"? Swedish troops have been among the first to go to Korea, the Congo, and other trouble spots to help maintain the peace. Sweden has built many wonderful hospitals in Norway and Denmark, neighboring countries that fought with the Allies and resented the neutrality of the Swedes. Individual Swedes, such as Count Folke Bernadotte, who died while trying to mediate peace in Palestine for the United Nations, and Dag Hammarskjold, Secretary-General of the United Nations, who died in an airplane crash while on his way to try to negotiate a cease-fire agreement in the Congo, are famous in current history for valiant efforts in behalf of world peace. Is it possible that nations like Ireland and Switzerland have tried to appease guilt feelings about remaining neutral in World War II through actions for peace now?

There are munitions makers in America who have started peace foundations. Some of the scientists who worked on the atom bomb have destroyed themselves or have become deeply involved in peace movements or acts of mercy. Remember old Scrooge in Dickens' famous "A Christmas

Carol"? He finally had such guilt feelings about hoarding his wealth and about being so cruel to others that he gave generously to people in need. Guilt in these instances caused actions that benefited mankind, which points up that guilt can serve a useful purpose in our lives!

When we feel the guiltiest, we sometimes give presents or pay for our guilt with money, gifts, and/or service. Much of this giving operates on levels within us that we are unaware of, and most of us would be insulted if we were told that guilt feelings were responsible for many of the nice and kind acts we perform. But have you ever had punitive thoughts toward your parents or some other older person and subsequently were more attentive to them or surprised them with some flowers or a gift, probably to make sure that nothing would happen to you or to them as a result of your thoughts? Some parents feel guilty about what they have not done in the way of giving love, interest, time, understanding, encouragement, effort, and security to their children. So they may flood their children with money, extra allowances, toys, and gifts. They often feel that they can make up by these means for what they have not done.

Countries do this too and have for many years—witness the reparations agreements between Germany and Israel, between Japan and a number of the countries in Asia. Some people feel that they can avoid punishment and gain social approval by giving to others when they feel guilty.

Sometimes when we feel guilty, we are the most self-righteous people. We all know people who were once the most ardent unbelievers and then became the most ardent believers, people who have been converted and who are far stricter than others of their group, people who have been guilty of vices and who have become the greatest reformers. The ex-criminal, the ex-drug addict, the ex-alcoholic, the ex-smoker, the ex-atheist, the ex-Communist, the ex-Fascist, the ex-anything can often be the hardest on his former group and the most zealous crusader for the "good" cause. Can that sometimes be true of the "ex-child"? And what about the "ex-infant"?

We most often punish ourselves when we feel guilty, and we find ingenious ways to do it. There are people who, without knowing it, punish themselves by becoming ill or subject to many accidents. We read in the newspapers of dishonest laborers or businessmen who try to escape paying taxes who suddenly have a heart attack when they are caught. When we feel guilty, some of us suffer from violent headaches or vomiting or diarrhea, which may get rid of everything but our guilt. Others suffer from skin disorders or rashes. Others fall down and hurt themselves, break a bone, or are left with a deep scar and have been known to say, "Well, I guess I am paying for all my sins with this!"

Sometimes parents and children use illness to encourage guilt feelings in one another and, in a way, punish one another. You have heard of the ill parent who demands extra attention just at the time that some independent activity is being launched by her child. You are no doubt also familiar with the sudden illness of a child whose parents were just ready to leave on holiday. None of us sits around and thinks up these diabolical ideas, but our guilt feelings refuse to stay submerged and seek expression.

Some people feel absolution by punishment. Spanking or a hard slap can make a child feel he has paid for his misdeed. He may continue to repeat the same act and pay for it each time with a smack or a belting. Parents are really the ones who feel guilty about spanking, not youngsters, because parents are relieved of their anger by hitting out but then worry about harming their youngster. Children often prefer a slap to that painful reproach quietly administered by a disappointed parent who lets you know you have not measured up to his high opinion of you. Children often prefer a spanking to having an activity or pleasure withheld or to being isolated, because they are often relieved of guilt feelings by being spanked and left with only a sore bottom.

Children often feel guilty and assume responsibility when their parents fight, separate, divorce, die. They often wrongly believe that a misfortune is the result of their own misdeeds and go through life overburdened with unnecessary and overwhelming guilt feelings and a need to punish themselves. Frequently they have felt that the impulsive angry feeling or the nasty thought that they directed against their parents was responsible for the disaster that occurred. It is not logical, but life rarely is logical, for we "feel" our way around more than we like to admit. If a child feels angry and has been taught his anger is bad, then he may attribute misfortunes to his own badness.

Those of us who are members of a minority group are quick to feel guilty at the slightest provocation due to our many fears and insecurities. We also may assume responsibility for deeds we did not do and add these guilt feelings to our pile. Members of a minority group often pick out the names and pictures of someone from their own minority who is in trouble and say: "Why did it have to be a Jew?" "Couldn't it have been someone other than a Negro!" "Why, of all people, did it have to be an Italian?" "If it only wasn't a Puerto Rican!" "Why did it have to be one of ours?"

We are often afraid when we feel guilty, and our fear gives rise to thoughts such as:

> Will the Lord punish me?
> Will those I love desert me?
> Will I poison everything I touch?

Will my guilt make me fail in all I do?
What evil will befall me?
Will I get sick and die?
What have I done to deserve all this?
Oh, God what will happen to me?

Do you feel guilty and afraid whenever you see a policeman? Do you feel guilty and afraid whenever you say "no"? Do you feel guilty and afraid when someone accuses you of something you have not done? Do you feel guilty whenever the older generation talks of the corruption, the delinquency, the tyranny of the younger generation?

Most young people are not guilty of delinquency, corruption, and tyranny. Most older people are not guilty of blaming all young people for most of society's woes. Those that do are usually the people who are most afraid of getting old and are least satisfied with their lives. They envy the many opportunities open to young people, particularly if they feel guilty that they never made much of their lives or never took proper advantage of opportunities offered them for growth, effort, and achievement. The older people who feel guilty about overindulgence in sexual affairs or about personal rigidity are among the first to condemn "our wanton youth" and to declare that promiscuity and violence never existed before. There are a number of older people who say that young people today are worse than ever before. In ancient times, the great philosopher Socrates said: "Our youth now loves luxury. They have bad manners, contempt for authority, disrespect for their elders. Children nowadays are tyrants."

Most older people are sympathetic to younger people and recognize that each generation has its own trials and tribulations, each is called the worst by the generation preceding it. The older generation in our country comes in for more criticism, challenging, and questioning than its counterpart in almost any other country. It is in our history, for our ancestors challenged beliefs to come here, challenged the ways of the past by separating from their families, overthrew the rule of the king—and thereby made it possible for us today to challenge the authority of our President and other elected leaders. Remember, Grandma was a rebel in her own way!

Older people draw upon great reservoirs of past experience and independent striving that we can profit from. We often feel guilty about the walls of silence between us and our elders that deprive us of the richness of their experiences and knowledge and keep us from knowing more about them. There is so very much that can make us feel guilty, but let us not forget that there is much that can make our parents feel guilty.

Besides all that we have discussed so far, there is a guilty feeling that all parents share and that you may share when you become a parent. Parents ask themselves, "Am I doing everything possible for my children to help them become the finest human beings they can?" Parents, like other people, are self-doubting and uncertain much of the time. Parenthood is no easy job. Most parents are aware of their limitations, and all parents feel inadequate in one area or another. They receive conflicting advice from all corners of their daily world and receive constant criticism from their parents, children, the educators, and the child-care experts.

Most parents try to give all they are capable of giving emotionally, socially, financially to their children. Some are more capable than others, and even the most capable of parents have frailties and weaknesses that make them feel guilty. Parents who were immigrants and parents from minority groups who have suffered some form of deprivation are all the more anxious to give as much as they can to their children to protect them from deprivation and to give them every chance in the world that they themselves may have been denied. With all the good intentions, all the giving, there can still be conflict between parents and children, because our parents' expectations of us often cannot be met by us, and we feel guilty, just as our expectations of our parents often cannot be met by them, and they feel guilty.

As long as we live, we shall be in situations that will make us feel guilty, and sometimes our guilt feelings will help us and sometimes they will hinder us, but we can learn to live with them. If we feel we cannot discover alone what we feel guilty about and why and if we fear that our guilt feelings are taking us over, we can relieve the heavy weight by seeking out and talking with someone who is in a position to help us.

6. Rivalry and Competition

How IMPORTANT do you feel it is to "win" all the time? Do you feel you must always "beat" the next guy? Do you feel upset if you are not "first" or "tops" in all that you do? Are you constantly busy with your inner ruler, measuring yourself against everybody else to see who is "best"? Do you have any brothers and sisters? Is it possible that you measure yourself against your brothers and sisters with your inner ruler?

Learning to live together in the intimate world of the family is our testing ground for later relationships. Cooperation and competition within our own families weigh heavily on our lives.

Ever since there has been a family, there has been cooperation and competition. Brothers and sisters through the ages have been loving and sharing, fighting and competing, grabbing and teasing, tattling and keeping secrets, agreeing and disagreeing, playing with and shunning one another. History and literature have recorded this. The Bible, Greek mythology, fairy tales, songs, dances, dramas illustrate the universality of the rivalries and tensions, as well as the harmony, that exist between brothers and sisters. No matter how loving the parents are, there is inevitably some rivalry between brothers and sisters, and there always will be. Why? Have you ever had something that was exclusively yours and then suddenly you had to share it? Did you have something that belonged to a few of you and then others came along who had to be included? Didn't you tend to feel a wee bit resentful? Each child in each family, regardless of how many other children there are, wants to be sure of the love and attention of his parents. It is difficult to learn that love for one does not mean less love for another, that opportunity for one does not necessarily mean less opportunity for another. Each child with brothers and sisters is forced to share his parents' love and attention. This is more painful for some children than for others. Even the only child must learn to share his mother with his father and his father with his mother.

Brothers and sisters provide each other with companionship as ready-made playmates, frequently share a sense of solidarity (sometimes consolidated against the parents), and they enjoy many opportunities to learn from one another. Often they feel pride about each other and respect. Growing up with brothers and sisters means a lot of give-and-take, constant frustrations, disappointments, hard knocks, challenges, and competition on a daily level. The only child is not deprived of frustrations, disappointments, challenges, especially when he is forced to learn from outside group situations what brothers and sisters learn to live with inside their families. Some of us learn to meet these demands without being beaten by them. Others look upon our family life as one big contest that we aim to win or that we feel we can never win.

The children who grow up feeling that their parents are rejected by society and don't have a fair chance in life sense the oppression of "my folks don't count and neither do I."

They often resign themselves to the same kind of life and never attempt anything better. When people don't know that life can be any better, there is little incentive to compete or to cooperate. The Arabs have one word that describes this attitude—and a shrug of the shoulders that accompanies it. It is *malesh,* which means that life is miserable, it always has been, it always will be, one life is just like another, so why worry or do anything about it. The moment that people see that life *can* be better, they are frustrated by what is not available to them. They may, at that point, strive to better their conditions and compete with others. Taking the initiative, making the effort, participating more in the world around them may be encouraged by competition, or it may be thwarted by competition.

Some of us need a certain amount of competition to encourage us to grow, develop, meet new challenges. Some of us are devastated by or shy away from any competition. Is competition itself a menace to our lives? Or is it the degree of competition, how we respond to it, and how it is used that can menace our lives? Is it when we feel in danger, threatened, that competition is unhealthy?

Excessive competition reflects an inner need to win, to be best, to knock someone else down, to outstrive, to outdo, to outstrip others, to achieve more and more, often in the end being less satisfied because our goals are never fully attainable. Excessively competitive people are often people who have never stopped struggling for supremacy over a brother or sister to achieve more love and approval from their parents and from others in authority. Deep down, they feel less worthy than a brother or sister. Often this feeling is translated into the more urgent need to prove to all people (authorities in particular) that they are worthy. One way to prove it is to excel. Even the child who has no brothers and sisters may strive to excel in order to prove his worth to his parents, when he doesn't feel safe and sure in his parents' esteem. When we feel worthy, we do not have the same need to prove to everyone that we are worthy.

According to his own account, T. E. Lawrence, the famed Lawrence of Arabia, was obsessed with the need to prove himself better than others, to prove that he could excel others in every possible way, through strength, speed, wit, cunning, and that he could withstand tortures of mind, body, and spirit that were superhuman. Why? Because he was the illegitimate son of Lord Chapman, a man whose wife would not give him a divorce when he ran off with their children's governess. The governess, whom he loved, bore Lord Chapman five sons. T. E. Lawrence was the second of these. Although neighbors said that Lord Chapman, his sons, and their mother lived a very intimate, affectionate, dignified family life, the shame that came from the knowledge of his illegitimacy apparently drove Lawrence of Arabia to prove his worth to the world.

Parents who are subjected to religious, racial, or other prejudices frequently drive themselves and their children to prove themselves "good" in order to protect themselves and their children from further prejudice, to win the battle for acceptance. These children may feel defeated by constantly having to prove themselves. Or when a child does drive himself too hard to prove that he can excel despite being a foreigner, a Negro, a Jew, an outcast, the other children may consider him a threat and exclude him for being the favored one, "a grind," or always at the top. When parents drive children, it is more than likely that the children may feel that they must be unworthy if they have to prove to their own parents that they are worthy!

When a child feels prized by his parents, not just for the

prizes he wins, but for the person he is, he feels worthy. Every child wants to be the nucleus of his world. It is less difficult for him to make room for others in his parents' affection when he feels sure of his home ground. Learning to share and cooperate in a family means giving up pleasures, privileges, space, time, furniture, clothing, toys, and countless other things.

When the atmosphere of our home is fairly tranquil and our parents seem to be in harmony, with Mother and Father seeming to live well with their differences, the ability of brothers and sisters to grow up more happily together, to cooperate and share, is promoted. The more well-fed we are emotionally, the more possible it is for us to turn "It's mine!" into "You may play with it for a while. We can take turns. We can all share it." But as cooperative as our natures generally are, none of us can do this all the time. Inevitably, there are moments when we feel that brothers and sisters are depriving us of what we want. We sometimes feel angry, resentful, and full of hatred when we are deprived of what we want.

The fear that our parents may not love us as much as they do the others creates the anger that we call jealousy. This jealousy and our guilt feelings about being jealous are all natural experiences of children growing up together in a family. But the extent to which these feelings prevail and dominate the whole atmosphere of the home, the way in which these feelings are dealt with, may make competition assume unnatural proportions in our lives.

Brothers and sisters need the help of their parents to build good relationships, for they do not have the experience to accomplish this by themselves. When parents create harmony and cooperation in the home, they offer many individual opportunities for development, encourage individual and special interests, build up skills, provide outside stimulation, work and play with their children, and know when to leave them alone. When parents encourage a sense of satisfaction and a delight in each child's efforts, they engender excitement and good feeling in their home.

A sympathetic and understanding ear, a ready hug, observing eyes, an inquisitive nose to sniff out what or who is causing trouble and why, a keen touch, an ability to keep tuned into family feelings—all help lessen uncomfortable competition in the home.

Anything that a parent can do to reinforce his child's confidence in himself promotes healthy relations in the family and outside. Parents are often tired, under strain, or upset. Under these conditions, they cannot consistently satisfy their children's needs, and children do bicker, quarrel, argue, and fight. But when parents can accept the imperfections of family life, their children learn to accept the imperfections of their parents. When parents attempt to channel negative feelings into the least harmful expressions, children are helped to handle more effectively the inevitable conflicts, tensions, rivalries, and deprivations of adult life. How do you respond to rivalries now? How do you think you will feel when you are a parent about your children's bickering, fighting, and competing? Do you think you will act in the same way that your parents do?

Many of our parents had brothers and sisters and have experienced rivalry and competition in their families. Their feelings about their brothers and sisters enter into their feeling about themselves, affect their feelings about us, and influence how they deal with our rivalries and competition.

Did our parents feel inferior to their brothers and sisters? Were they teased a lot or ignored by their brothers and sisters? Were they punished for beating up or undermining their brothers and sisters? Did they tend to feel defeated by competition in their families? When people feel defeated by competition in their families, every competitive situation can become a threat to them, because it confirms their low opinions of themselves. The parents who fear competition may be the very parents who condemn their children's rivalry and competitive attitudes.

All parents get fed up with their children's constant bickering, and all parents have to call a stop to it. Often children depend upon their parents to tell them "Enough!" Children need help in controlling themselves, and a limit has to be set to name-calling and negativism. All parents go about it differently, but there are some similarities in what they say when their children are quarreling. Listen:

Stop fighting this minute!
I'm going to punish you for quarreling.
You are basically mean, all of you!
I don't ever want to hear you talk to each other like that again!
Apologize to your sister and tell her you love her.
Do you want to kill one another? Then go ahead!
You must never hate each other. You must love each other.
You disgrace our whole family by your fighting.
There is something wrong with brothers and sisters who don't love each other.
No one will like you if you don't help each other.
I will punish you if I ever hear you say anything against your brothers and sisters.
I won't stand for another minute of this picking on one another!
Can't you ever say a nice word to each other?
You're doing it just to upset me!

How can you do this to me? Don't you love me? I can't stand any more of this!

Does any of this sound familiar? If parents consistently refuse to listen to a child's negative feelings, these negative feelings about himself and others are reaffirmed. He learns to deny rivalries and hatreds and shoves them underground. His negative feelings about his brothers and sisters will not lie dormant but will pop into other relationships. Sometimes, without realizing it, his life becomes populated with brothers and sisters. If he does not become aware of his feelings or receive help from others, throughout his life he may still be fighting his childhood battles and may act angry toward the whole world or become excessively competitive or withdrawn. Or he may become excessively "nice" on the surface.

Most parents try to encourage their children to be "nice" to one another. They have to! But some parents are overly concerned with the impressions their children make on others and how others value them. These parents place great emphasis on surface niceness, since it speaks well for the job they have done in rearing their children. The niceties and politenesses do help make the world a pleasanter place. The "please's" and the "thank you's" can make us more willing to do things for others. But sometimes "niceness" and "good behavior" are not genuine and are used not only to compete with brothers and sisters for more approval and acceptance from parents but also to win over others.

Surface niceness may be used to conceal a girl's seething anger and resentment, and she may go through life feeling "nice" and miserable. Because the "good" child causes no problem for parents and teachers, she is often patted on the back and then quickly ignored. Often they are surprised to find that this same girl may be unhappy inside and are shocked when she suddenly does something destructive. Children who are extremely well-behaved when an authority is around sometimes go wild when left without supervision. The "good" child must not be overlooked, because she may have more problems than the boisterous child or even the "bad" child!

The so-called bad, naughty child reflects her feelings about herself through her actions. She may feel that her parents, brothers, and sisters consider her "no good," so she lives up to her reputation. To attract the attention of her brothers and sisters, she may be a "pest," a "brat," a "first-class nuisance," a "pain in the neck." Most of us would rather get into trouble than be ignored. Surely you know of a younger brother or sister who will not leave the older ones alone and asks for trouble because he or she wants so desperately to be included.

When brothers and sisters grow up and reminisce about their childhood, frequently they find that they envied each other and are surprised that the others shared so many of their feelings, worries, unhappinesses. Each position in a family has its privileges as well as its drawbacks. Do you think there is an ideal position?

"Oh, if I were only the eldest, I would have so many more privileges!" we often say. The eldest does tend to receive more attention and adoration from his parents because he is the first child. But he also receives more of his parents' insecurities and anxieties—parenthood is new to them. The oldest child frequently benefits from special attention and unusual opportunities. But he often believes he has the worst deal because he is asked to assume the most responsibility. Because of their lack of experience, new parents expect their first child to live up to unrealistically high standards. The oldest child was the only child for a while—and he never forgets it! It is often more difficult for him to share, to stop being bossy, to relinquish demands than it is for the children who follow him. They are born *having* to share parents' time, attention, and love with the older child.

"Well, I wish I were the second, because they have an easier life!" The second child (or, in a large family, others who are not the youngest) has more secure and less anxious parents who are more comfortable in the parental seat. He is usually given more freedom and allowed to do things at an earlier age than the oldest. But the second child has the model of the older one as an example to follow. He continually tries to keep up with the older one (particularly if they are close in age) and is frequently frustrated by having to run to catch up. He tends to think he has the worst deal in the family. He receives less attention and is catered to less than the oldest. A little healthy neglect sometimes hastens his self-reliance. However, if his parents feel very disappointed or upset with the elder child, they become anxious and make heavy demands on the second. There is no one pattern, but there are some similarities in how parents treat their first-born, middle, and youngest.

"Oh! to be the youngest! That's the good life!" we often hear. The youngest child frequently receives a lot of attention from parents and older brothers and sisters. He is frequently allowed privileges, opportunities, and freedom either denied the others or given at a later stage. But the youngest child may feel that *he* has the worst deal because he is often frustrated by a double standard: he is treated like a baby yet expected to live up to what the rest of the family is doing. He learns a great deal from his brothers and sisters but is often left out or left at home because he is too young.

All children suspect their parents of showing favoritism at one time or another. First in the family or last, we make endless demands on our parents, are frequently rebuffed by them, and resent their fulfilling the demands of our brothers and sisters:

> Why did you give it to him, and not to me?
> What did she do to deserve that?
> You have to give something to me too!
> You are always doing things for him!
> She always gets everything!
> You don't treat me the same!

Frequently we complain that we do not receive equal treatment from our parents and that they don't treat us all the same. But do we really want them to treat us all the same? Can they? Parents feel differently about each child. This depends on what happens in their lives before the child is born, the conditions of pregnancy and childbirth, what happens when the child is growing up. Each parent treats each child differently because each child is different. Even identical twins react differently, have different potentials, talents, ideas, interests, and unique mannerisms. Each child needs different things, warrants different approaches, and has different qualities to offer.

Feeling differently about each child or treating each one differently does not necessarily mean favoritism. For some parents, it may imply favoritism. But for others, spending more time with one child during certain periods or encouraging one, inhibiting another, or keeping hands off another does not add up to their favoring one more or loving one more. When a child knows he can depend upon his parents to come to him when he needs them, he can understand and accept their giving attention to a brother or sister who may need it. When he feels that he cannot count on them, he resents all attentions given to others.

We often think that being treated the same means equality. To treat people exactly the same when they are not the same is not equality. Equality means respect for differences. Fair treatment means equal opportunity for all, but each individual person need not take the same path, do the same things, act the same way. Cooperation thrives on differences in ability, experience, and purpose. Respect for differences is an essential booster of good relations between brothers and sisters. Parents who respect themselves tend to respect each other's individuality and tend to encourage their children's individuality and respect for each other.

When parents can help us learn within our own families to accept differences and respect them, we are likely to have better relations later on with others from all walks of life, of all races, religions, nationalities. When differences are acceptable at home, then the bigger differences among people are acceptable to us, and we don't tend to pick on the handicapped, crippled, and retarded for something they cannot help. Three-year-olds often observe out loud the differences they see in people. Most of them observe in a nonjudgmental way, but some feel the need to belittle others for having a large belly button, tiny ears, a lisp, a deformity of some kind. It is frequent that the children who tease other children because they are different (handicapped in walking, in using their arms or in seeing, hearing, speaking, learning) have learned at home that differences are unacceptable.

The child who is handicapped physically or neurologically, or is a member of a minority race or religion, may be helped at home to feel at peace with his differences. He may be less handicapped emotionally than the child with no overt handicaps. When a child feels the need to use his handicaps or differences as an excuse for not competing, he may say, "I can't do it; it's unfair," when, in reality, he is indeed capable of competing. He may take unfair advantage of others by using these excuses to "get ahead." He may play on the guilt feelings of those around him so that they will favor him, which is why sometimes a poorly qualified person has been elected to school office or given a job. Do you feel you cannot ever say anything against anyone in a minority group or against a handicapped person? Is this not a way of denying differences? How do you react to people who are different from you? Do you feel you are not treated fairly in your family or in general? Even when we are not subjected to some form of discrimination or prejudice, some of us never cease saying, "It's not fair," because we continually feel cheated and deprived. This may be because we continue to feel "beaten" by brothers and sisters or because we don't feel loved and respected by our parents.

Our parents may feel that they love us and respect us, but something may have gone wrong in the transmission of these feelings. There are some parents who express their frustrations with their own lives by showing great favoritism, by concentrating on one child to the exclusion of the others, by setting up one as a model for the rest, by treating all their children as opponents in a family shooting match. Carrying a sense of parental injustice through life may jeopardize a man's career, a woman's marriage, a person's ability to have fun.

You have no doubt heard of the famous political and military strategy of "divide and conquer." The British used this technique effectively in the days of colonialism in order to maintain control and encourage dependence. It is said that they played the Muslims off against the Hindus and encouraged competition and rivalry between them so that the British would stay on top. Some parents do this when they constantly compare, judge, and rate one child by the performance of the others. They expect each child to have all the desirable traits of the others. Such demands cause each child to feel less worthy and can encourage dependence on parents. This treatment weakens a child's cooperation with and respect for another, because it ignores the individual personality, abilities, and interests of each child.

All parents make comparisons at times, encourage some competition in the hope of stimulating more effort or because they want something done in a hurry. But some parents have excessive needs to be "best," "first," and "on top." They are constantly comparing themselves with their neighbors, and how they feel about themselves (and their children) is determined by how well they feel the competition is going. In the families where life is a race to the finish line, the following questions become terribly important:

Who's the best behaved in this family today?
Who will finish breakfast first?
Which one will be dressed first?
Who will get her job done first?
Who is the best helper?
Who is the best finder?
Who won a prize at the playground?
Who looks the prettiest today?

Who is the cleanest today?

Let's see, which one of you has the best report card?

Are you at the top of the class?

Who is the most popular in your group?

Who is the best athlete?

Who do you like better?

What do you like best?

Who's best?

Why can't you be like your sisters and brothers?

Why can't you ever be first?

Will you ever do anything better than anyone else?

We all use these phrases to one degree or another. How much? How meaningful are they to us? Do we score ourselves and others according to how we came out in the competition at home, at school, in sports, with friends, for dates, at work? Should we? Are we ever ashamed of our brothers and sisters because they are not "tops"? Do we tend to criticize them and others more than we praise?

When children in a family are quick to attack each other for clumsiness, mistakes, failures and are very slow to praise each other for trying, for accomplishing something, we can assume that they don't feel very sure of themselves. Should we also assume that their parents have not made them feel praiseworthy? When older children baby-sit, they reflect the methods and attitudes they have learned from their parents. Some of us know only negative methods for managing younger children, because these are what we ourselves are used to. "No, that's naughty! You'll be punished if you take that away from her! Shame on you! Can't you ever do anything right?" is the way some parents handle difficulties with children. "That's not a good idea. Let's see what we can do about it. Give that back to her, please, and we can see what else you can play with. Good girl! Gee, you did that nicely!" is how others handle the same situation. Why? What have they learned?

Some parents regulate the praise and attention they give their children according to the degree of achievement and competitive gain their children attain. They may not mean to do it, but many parents are more loving with their children when they have done well and less affectionate when their children have failed at something. Sometimes the reverse is true. When we are "down and out," we most need the encouragement and faith of our parents. We need them to love us for the people we are, not just for what we have done and how we have performed.

In our country, how we have performed is considered of the utmost importance. We are a nation of "doers," and what we do, how fast we do it, and where it leads us are highly emphasized. Perhaps this goes way back to the beginnings of our country, when Europeans left roots and security, often to escape persecution and injustice, to seek new opportunities in a new country in which they hoped to create a better world for themselves. Conditions were difficult, and what was "done" was important, and there was a short time to do it in. America was built largely on pioneer achievements, initiative, autonomy, speed, which guaranteed the early settlers a better chance for survival.

Speed is very important to us. The early settlers were in a hurry, and we have continued to be in a hurry. Unlike the older nations of the world, where a job well done counts more than speed (and where progress may be slower), we are concerned with how fast we can do things and whether we can do them faster than someone else. Parents are extremely concerned with how early an infant sits, how soon she learns to walk and move around by herself, how early she begins to talk. Our children are encouraged to eat by themselves early, to look and act grown up as fast as possible. Yet just as we rush our children to grow up, we advise our older people to stay young and "hide those nasty wrinkles," "dye those gray hairs," feel young, think young, act young! Have you noticed this?

Our emphasis on speed presumably grew out of a goal to "get somewhere," "be somebody," "do better than the next guy." Our economic system encourages us to produce faster than the next guy, and incentives are given for outproducing the next guy. This has brought about a great deal of progress for our country, but sometimes at a personal cost to its people. It has increased frustration for those people who are not allowed (for example, because of race) to steam ahead and engage in hot competition.

Mobility is deeply rooted in our tradition. The westward movement across our country is only one example of this. Americans are always on the move. Many of us have been and continue to be constantly on the move for betterment. The "past" and very little mobility are deeply rooted in the traditions of most other countries. Children are encouraged to live in the same home town as their parents, carry on the same traditions with their own children, with the generations of families remaining in very close touch. American children are raised "to make do" anywhere, to be flexible, enterprising, on the move, with the generations dispersing. According to statistics, at this time next year, one out of every five Americans will be living in a different home. Many parents tell their children that they can "be President," that "the world is your oyster," that "the sky is the limit," that they must seek new opportunities and make the most of them. We all know of men who had been deprived of economic and educational advantages yet who became President of our country, leaders in business, and tops in the professional world. Americans move economically as well as geographically.

To "get ahead" for more money, more prestige, more status, what some of us call more security, has been a driving force in our country. To get ahead despite how you get ahead has confused our morality. We tend to rate people as successful or unsuccessful, more successful or less successful, or more or less successful. Notable achievement is widely used to measure a person's worth.

There is a tremendous premium on achieving good grades in school and not enough emphasis on learning. Is this premium partly responsible for the large number of dropouts? Certainly there are some students who must leave school in order to support their families and others who are getting married or are having babies. But researchers have discovered that students who depart before graduating are almost always those who are working below their own capacities, are not doing well in studies, and are rarely participating in school activities. Usually these same students are afraid of failing, are threatened by competition. If you have brothers and sisters who tease you and foster your low opinion of yourself, wouldn't it follow that if you started out convinced that you could not do well, the competition of schoolmates would further convince you of your worthlessness? And couldn't we take that one step further and say that because everything so far has been a failure, you might think there is no use trying to do any better? So you quit school and join the legion of unemployed.

Far too frequently we condemn those students who are failing in high school, but didn't try to help them in the early years when they showed the need for more special attention and help in such subjects as reading. We neglect to give praise for those things they do well, and we neglect to encourage them toward what they might do well. So their failures accumulate, they are always behind, and they feel defeated. Dropping out of school usually is a symptom of a problem that has been building up over a long period of time. Because this problem was unattended in the early years, a person and our country are deprived of education and self-confidence that could help the person achieve his capacity and contribute more to all of us. Perhaps our schools need to keep their eyes less on group norms and more on individual students. Doing so would decrease competitive pressures.

We place so much emphasis on achieving and winning in our country that we often overlook those who nearly won and treat them as failures or ignore them altogether. Presidential candidates who nearly won the nomination are not congratulated and revered for being competent enough to have been a candidate, but are pitied or criticized for failing. The same holds true in the workaday world. In school, in scholastic contests, second and third best are ignored or often written off as also-rans, as are those in the bottom half of an "honors" group. Do we treat with respect the paper that nearly hung on the bulletin board, the poem that almost got into the school paper, the painting that didn't quite make the school exhibition? Do we enjoy athletics as much as we could if we were not always bent on winning and being the champs?

Starting in the preschool years, many children lose the joy of playing games, being with one another, laughing, hiding, romping around, because the goal of being "first," having to win, has been superimposed on their play. Athletic competition is fun when the underlying spirit is to have a good time—to have fun with teammates and to get to know them better—and when team spirit is as important as winning. But when every competitive sport is taken as a personal challenge to win or lose, then we lose a relaxation and a pleasure. If you have had a good time, does it matter if you lose? If you have worked hard to perfect a skill over a period of time, it does matter when you lose, but does it mean that you are "no good"?

In our country, we almost make a fetish of the winner. We laud him with praise, honors, medals, money, and glory. We blow him up to fantastic proportions and in many instances soon forget him. We rarely honor the runners-up and seldom draw attention to the skills of all those who competed in a contest. In Europe, a man who is talented, a professional who is good enough to enter a high-level competition, is widely admired for that. If he is not the winner, he is still revered for his skill and rare achievement. In the famous Tour de France bicycle race, all contestants (even the one who comes in last) who finish the twenty-two-day 2,654-mile race are given honors and flowers. All top-level European automobile racers are given prizes and hailed as champions. Every great European athlete (or team) is treated with respect, and they don't lose that when they fail to be the winners. There are no winners in the annual four-day walking marathon (the Vierdaagse) that takes place in the Netherlands. Thousands of hikers from all over the world take part in it for the fun of walking. They receive inexpensive medals as prizes for covering the long distances in the allotted four days.

Do you tend to treat the champion team or person who wins as a success and all the others as failures? Are you inspired by your parents, teachers, by the country in general to give proper credit to the effort, the perseverance and

We Americans blow up our heroes to fantastic proportions and then forget about them shortly thereafter.

patience, the development of skill and rare achievement that the losers show?

Young people today are widely criticized for wanting Cadillacs without working for them, wanting fast miracles and instant successes. We are criticized for not wanting to make the effort, for not recognizing the efforts of our elders, for not appreciating the extraordinary efforts that have made our country what it is today. But young people are growing up in a country that preaches effort, but advertises the glories of not making an effort. Take a magazine that has wide circulation and study its advertisements. You will see these words and phrases: *instant, ready-mixed, pre-cooked, effortless, no bother, no fuss, takes no time.* They are considered to be great selling points. Think about auto-mation, automatic brains, computers, and other mechanical devices that many businesses are using because they are faster and, some say, more efficient than human beings. Then add to these enticements for not exerting effort the pressures in our country hurrying young people to grow up and "be" something. Is it then such a wonder that many of us want to take short cuts, the quick way, the ready-mixed results? Is it surprising that we learn to cut corners and save time, bother, and effort? The success schools, the charm schools, and other such schools that promise to change us overnight, just like the pills, diets, and chewing gum that promise we will lose weight all of a sudden, mis-lead us into thinking sometimes that we can get away with doing as little as possible and still obtain good results. The vast competitive atmosphere that we live in, where we are rarely treated as the people we are, but mostly for what we can produce, tends sometimes to prevent us from making an effort.

Many visiting Asians have remarked that Americans are

too critical of themselves and each other and seem very defensive about making mistakes. Some of us treat each mistake as though it were a sin. A mistake often becomes an indictment of a person, proof of his inadequacies, an admission of failure rather than an acknowledgement of human fallibility. We tend to look upon mistakes with impatience because they take up precious time when we are intent on quick results. But how do we learn? We learn things by experience, by making mistakes. It is difficult to learn from the mistakes of others. Young people, just like young countries, need and want the right to make their own mistakes and learn from them. There are certain steps, stages, and phases of experience that we cannot skip or glide over but that can be learned only through trial and error. The newcomer nations often want to skip processes and steps necessary to development, but they find that they cannot avoid mistakes. They too have discovered that mistakes can be useful in growing, learning, finding new ways, changing our ways, stumbling onto progress.

Parents make mistakes. If they didn't, they would not be human. Some parents make a superhuman effort to hide their mistakes, because they feel guilty about making mistakes, because they feel they should be perfect. If parents feel guilty about making mistakes it is likely that their children feel guilty about making mistakes. Parents and children who feel guilty about making mistakes never admit making mistakes, exaggerate the consequences of the mistakes of others, minimize their mistakes, or blame their mistakes on someone else.

Parents launch children on the way to honest appraisals of themselves by acknowledging, examining, admitting, and looking at their own mistakes. They are thus relieved of having to pretend to an adequacy they don't possess. At the same time, both parents and children acquire more self-confidence in knowing mistakes can be made and can be built upon constructively. When a parent can discuss her own shortcomings with her children, she demonstrates that she knows the areas of her competence and is proud of them. She shows that she is aware of areas of her incompetence and failure and can try to do something about them. In turn, her child can dare to have an estimate of her strengths and weaknesses. She can feel a certain security about what she can do and is less devastated by what she is unable to do. This lessens her need to belittle others.

We all face frustrations and will continue to face them throughout our lives. We learn to tolerate frustration (and making mistakes can be frustrating) by experiencing frustration, looking at it, and forcing ourselves to go on. There is no ingredient more essential to our self-confidence than effort. "I can do it! I did it! It's good! I made it!" we say with pride when we know we have put real effort into something. Sometimes when we really try, we are surprised at our own capabilities. Sometimes our mistakes lead us to attempts and discoveries that enhance our lives.

Are you and your parents generous enough with time to allow you to make mistakes without condemnation? Can we expect ourselves and our parents to ignore the expectations, pressures, and values of our society? Whether we are aware of it or not, there is some degree of conflict in every family about what the outside world demands and wants and what the individual family members need and want. Conflict that normally exists between children in the same family for parental love and approval is not exactly helped by competition in the neighborhood for group approval, competition in school for good grades, competition on the athletic field for sporting honors, competition in the working world, in business, in professional life, and in politics for more status, prestige, and money—and always more achievements. What are the real achievements for us?

Isn't one of the real achievements for our parents, and for us eventually, to help children attain the self-respect needed in order to develop as fully as possible as human beings? Doesn't competition encourage our efforts in this direction when we can take it seriously but not let it govern us and drive us into an endless series of contests? How can we achieve enough of a comfortable feeling about ourselves to help our children feel less like contestants in life?

Parents whose antennae are in tune, who can listen to their children and hear the words and the feelings behind the words, are usually able to communicate with their children. Communication is indispensable to cooperation. Participation and sharing in family plans help all family members to feel that their opinions count. Usually the parents who value their children's opinions on many issues are the parents who tend to value their children even when they are acting their worst or are failing or are in trouble. The children who feel unlistened to, unheard, out of communication, tend to believe that their opinions are valueless anyhow, and if they do not withdraw from it all with a defeated sigh, they may try to express their worth through excessive competition.

The young people who feel defeated, the brothers and sisters who rival each other may be the brothers and sisters who rival the world for more attention and more approval, for more awards and more honors, for more money and more status—and are their own worst rivals!

7. Popularity and Conformity

EVERY SINGLE ONE of us wants to be liked. We all want to feel we belong. We all want others to respond positively to us. We all want the people we like to like us and to respond enthusiastically toward us. It is natural for us to want to be well-liked.

The popularity that will be explored in this chapter is not the popularity that is the natural desire we all share to be liked by others. The popularity we are probing is the overwhelming drive for universal acceptance and approval. Popularity, in this sense, is a striving for goals that can never be reached, because we can never be liked by everyone, please everyone, and be accepted by everyone.

There are differences in the way we relate to different people and in our relationships within the different groups we belong to. There are differences in the intensity of feeling and in the quality of feeling that we have for different people. It is impossible to have intense, deep relationships with multitudes of people.

Usually, each of us is accepted by someone, and it is rare that one of us is unaccepted by everyone. Just as financial success has become an end in itself to many people and a quantity of material possessions vital, so popularity has become an end in itself to many of the same people and a quantity of friends and acquaintances vital. If you measure popularity by the quantity of friends you have, clubs you belong to, invitations you receive, parties you attend, positions you attain, or people who know you by name, then popularity has to do with numbers, with quantity, rather than with quality and with feelings. Then popularity has to do with the extent of our relationships, with the width rather than the depth of relationships. Popularity, in this sense, has little to do with friendship.

Most of us are brought up by our parents to be flexible, adjustable, to be prepared for a mobile life, to fit into any group quickly and easily. As mentioned earlier, America is a land of great mobility; we do not count on living in the same place, seeing the same people the rest of our lives as others do in other countries. We are educated for mobility. Some of us are loners who never have more than a couple of friends and who keep close to ourselves, particularly when in a new situation. Many of us protect ourselves from getting hurt by surrounding ourselves with people whom we do not become deeply involved with. Others adjust easily to new situations and are able to fit into new groups quickly and to establish, in time, a few close friendships.

It is more important to some of us to achieve a certain popularity than it is to others. If to be popular you always have to have a smile on your well-scrubbed face, primp and fuss over yourself for hours, make a large investment in telephone calls, spend hours sitting and talking with people whom you don't even care about in order to keep your fingers on the pulse of activities and to be sure that you don't miss out on the latest fads and fancies—are you not

involved in a frantic race? Aren't you then directing tremendous energies and efforts toward the goal of popularity?
Aren't you compelled to deny yourself attention and to
neglect some of your own interests and development because of this striving for popularity? To be overly concerned
about being popular involves constant vigilance and takes a
disproportionate amount of time, effort, and persistence.
It is possible for people to be well-liked without making
popularity an all-consuming preoccupation. Their desire to
be liked is in proportion with other desires and aspirations.
They are able to be well-liked and yet maintain an independent spirit. The number of people who like them is
presumably less important than the quality of their relationships.

If you have warm, satisfying relationships with a few
people, why do you feel you need more? Often we wish to
enlarge our acquaintanceships in order to enlarge our
knowledge of what we like and the kind of people we like.
New people can introduce us to new ways of living, new
ideas, and the experience of coming to know them may
confirm our friendships with the people we already know
and like. It is natural for us to explore new friendships, but
is it natural to want applause and admiration from numbers
of people, even those we don't care about?

There are some of us who feel loved and don't need to be
surrounded by a mass of approving people. Others of us
tend to feel loved only when we are admired by numbers
of people, and we feel unloved if ignored by a quantity
of people. Since some people feel unable to achieve
genuine, secure relationships with a few people, they may
seek popularity as a substitute. Some actresses and actors
have declared that the applause and approval of an audience convey love and friendship to them. When they leave

the glow of the theater lights, they return to their own lives often feeling inadequate and unhappy, but sometimes bolstered by memories of audience applause and the glory accorded them. Was this part of the Marilyn Monroe story perhaps? Some theater people say they feel alive only with an audience responding to them. Some socially popular people feel the same way when there is an audience for them.

There are some people who are popular just because they feel comfortable inside themselves, and others sense their inner strength. These people are concerned about and for others. Their concern for others is part of the reason they are so well-liked. They put others at ease and are able to share with others the worries, the troubles, as well as the joys, in living. On the other hand, there are many socially popular people who are not willing or able to give significantly of themselves. There are those who do not genuinely care for those who admire them and do not give attention to the needs, concerns, and problems of others. Why? They are too often too busy measuring the impressions they are making on others to focus on anyone but themselves. It is interesting that "popularity" can include both kinds of people, or does it really?

What do you consider to be the generally accepted standards of popularity? Does popularity have to do with the person you are, or is what is important the way you look, general attractiveness, dash of style? Does a fair complexion, the color of your hair, or attractive body build assume importance? What about neatness? What about enthusiasm, a sense of humor, and general gaiety? Is it necessary to be outgoing, to have a smiling friendliness, poise, and flexibility? Is it necessary to demonstrate competence not only socially but in sports, in fighting, in dancing? Does it contribute if you do well in your studies, or does that hinder popularity? Is it helpful to be artistic or talented? Is prominent participation in extracurricular activities vital to popularity? Is it important to be involved in church groups and neighborhood groups as well as school groups? Is it necessary to be multifaceted, to have a multitude of skills, interests, and connections? Is it important to demonstrate a certain affluence through possessing certain material things? Does money have anything to do with popularity?

What does all this add up to and mean? Perhaps it adds up to conforming to particular standards and goals that glorify various features of a person rather than considering the individual person as a whole.

Is the socially popular boy or girl in your class necessarily a happy, contented, thoughtful, kind, imaginative, productive person? Not necessarily, but sometimes this can be so. However, it is not unusual that some of the most popular boys and girls in high school do not turn out to be extraordinary adults and may not even enjoy the deep contentment and rich fulfillment of many of the others in the class who were not particularly popular. Sometimes, personal growth can be thwarted by the concentration of time and effort that a person directs toward becoming socially popular and maintaining that popularity.

Do you think you are unpopular? Does this worry you and upset you? Do you tend to feel that the popular people you know "have everything" and that you are woefully lacking in almost everything? Do you tend to feel that since you are not popular, you are not worthwhile? Look up some of these socially popular people in about ten years and evaluate what it all means then. To your surprise, you may find that you worried an awful lot about something that really was not all that important. What is important is how

you can live your life to develop as fully as possible and
how your relationships with others enhance growth. Being
able to relate to others comfortably, being able to have
good friends and maintain friendships, is essential. Achieving popularity is not essential to your growth, although ad-
mittedly it is nice if it comes naturally and without a cam-
paign on your part.

Do you feel uncomfortable and ill at ease when you are
in the company of persons whom you consider to be important and advantageous to associate with? Do you feel
relaxed and that you can be yourself with a few people
whom you consider to be your good friends? If you genuinely like and enjoy being with a few friends who return your affection, then it is important for you to enjoy
more time with them and less time with the people who
make you feel uncomfortable. In this instance, perhaps we
need to cater to ourselves by letting ourselves enjoy our
comfort more.

It takes courage that grows out of security and confidence
to be strong enough to remain outside the race for popularity. To stand alone frequently precipitates teasing and
criticism for being different, for thinking differently. Not
actively contesting for popularity or not caring about being
popular with everyone is often equated with peculiarity. Do
you know what *peculiarity* means? It means distinctive,
unusual, unique. Peculiarity emphasizes that each of us is
different. Yet many of us consider it wrong to be unique,
different, so we use the word *peculiar* in a very derogatory
fashion. We use it to mean odd and queer instead of unique.
To stand with but a few friends, away from the race for
popularity, may bring us some unpleasantness and trouble-
some moments. But it can also bring us the deep respect and
trust of a few people and more self-respect.

It takes courage, inner strength, and some insight to be able to differ from the majority in what we believe and in what we individually wish to do. It is the line of least resistance to tag along after the crowd. To join in negative appraisals of others or to criticize usually does not require the same inner fortitude and conviction as to speak up *for* something. To stand alone, to propose a unique approach, or to challenge accepted concepts or ways of doing things is not easy. The true meaning of our beliefs and of the words we use is expressed through our actions, by the very way we live our lives.

"What will other people think of me?" Do you say this often to yourself and feel overly concerned about what others think of you? Do you conduct your own private opinion poll of what the reactions of others will be before you feel it is safe to go ahead and do something? Do you continue the poll afterward? Are you impelled to conform to what other people think is best, even when it is against your own interests or desires? What do you learn from the way your parents live their lives? Is conformity to their image of "success" their watchword?

For our own physical and emotional survival and to protect the best interests of the majority of people, we must cooperate with others and conform to certain standards. Sometimes after weighing a situation, we decide to conform. Other times, we feel driven to conform against our own inner dictates. Our lives are usually an infinitely varied mixture of conforming and dissenting, leading and following, accepting and denying, acting, compromising, remaining still. There are times when we have little choice and must conform. Other times we can use our judgment to decide whether or not to conform, where and when to conform.

It is difficult to go against the crowd.

The pressures of public opinion have always existed and will continue to exert pressures on us to conform.

When there is intense competition and fervent striving to get ahead, as there is in our country, then each step upward is marked by increasing pressure to fit into each new group, to become molded into the person that others want us to be. Conformity to the fashions and modes of public opinion has often become the price of success. Public opinion can become the dictator tyrannizing many of us.

"What other people think" has molded the way many of us live our lives, even though some deep probing into our own ideas and feelings might lead us in other directions. The parents who threaten children with "what other people think" may be the parents who are threatened by what other people think, for it is public opinion that influences them, that declares you successful or unsuccessful.

Many of the very great people throughout history have at times found it impossible to conform to the prevailing standards and beliefs. They have usually been people who expounded unusual concepts, people who dared to experiment and inaugurate new ways of doing things. Christopher Columbus was looked upon with scorn because he believed the world was round and that he could sail around it. He was laughed at, considered peculiar, rejected by the "crowd" until he had proven his beliefs. Many philosophers, scholars, artists, scientists, and ordinary thinking human beings who have changed the course of our lives and have brought us beauty, conveniences, and progress did not conform to the prevailing winds of public opinion. Yet we did and we do reject people who are different, who think differently, act differently, and do not fit into the mold that is in fashion in our society. Why?

In our country, the symbols of success that are usually valued by the public are:

dollars and cents
cars and big homes
television sets and fur coats
a quantity of material possessions
a quantity of associations
a quantity of friends
the position and status of a person and his family

Every country has goals that are valued by most of the people. The people who achieve these goals may be rewarded for their accomplishment with tattoos, special robes and decorations, scholastic honors, opportunities to be professors, special living quarters, property, a certain authority, unique privileges, jewelry, or money. When these symbols of achievement become goals in themselves, the original goals and values tend to be forgotten. Material possessions are easily seen, but the hard work, difficult decisions, patience, and perseverance that created the wealth are rarely appreciated in our society. Real status is usually based on achievements and not on the lucky get-rich-quick schemes that may have worked here and there for a few people.

The students in one high school who achieved A or A-minus averages in their last year of school were given watches by the principal. One girl who had achieved a B-plus average craved for a watch like the others. Her parents, who were used to indulging her, found out what type of watch the principal had purchased and bought one exactly like it for her. She wore it proudly and pretended she was one of the special in-group. But could she really feel proud inside herself? Did that watch mean to her that she was a worthwhile person, or did it in time move her to realize she was a phony?

On a larger scale, we often erect an untrue image or an exaggerated image to ensure our acceptance into a group of our choice. We may do it through wild spending of money, through driving cars or motorcycles, through waving diplomas and academic medals, through cigarettes, drink, or clothing. If we value ourselves according to how others value us, and if they value us according to our outward signs of success, our value of ourselves can only be unsubstantial. To depend upon the opinions of others alone for our self-esteem means that each day we have to convince others that we are O.K., and the overwhelming effort that demands is exhausting. If our fear of social disapproval and our fear of failure are so great that we feel that the source of all good is outside ourselves, then are we not becoming slaves to people and to things outside ourselves?

The Greek philosopher Plato once commented that a slave is one who gets his purpose from somebody else. In a sense, we are slaves when we are completely controlled, manipulated, driven into conformity by the dictates of public opinion, by "what other people think," by forces outside ourselves.

We deny the very value of a human being when our feeling of worth is equated with money and when our personal success is measured by the quantity of our material possessions. Money is indeed important for securing the basic necessities of life. The fact that money is used almost universally as a means of exchange demonstrates the need for it. And in this world, most people find it important to have. But some people hunger for money, like to accumulate it, fondle it, and spend their lives in pursuit of it. Their appetites never seem to be satiated. This can be true of those who have known poverty as well as those who have never been deprived of money. To some people, their own feeling of worth is all wrapped up in the quantity of paper and metal they possess. To them, financial failure, even when due to circumstances beyond their control, represents personal bankruptcy.

Money is like food. We need some of it to keep us alive and healthy. But craving more money, always more, regardless of need, can harm us, because money can have a dehumanized power over us. Instead of nourishing us, it can bring us discomfort, indigestion, constant dissatisfaction, because our appetites can keep stretching.

Since money is an essential part of our lives, our attitudes and feelings may often revolve around money. Money is important in family living and in family relationships. We all have to deal with it in our families, and different families deal with money in different ways. Our parents' attitudes about money are the primary source of our attitudes about money.

Excessive spending, excessive hoarding, unwise spending, losing of money, disgust over money are all manifestations of strong feelings within us. Some parents use money to represent love. If parents feel unable to give love or feel that their love for their children is inadequate, they may try to make up for this through smothering a child with gifts, with toys, and with money. If parents feel guilty about not giving a child the love and attention they think they should be giving, they may try to use money to demonstrate the love. Many "poor little rich girls" know only too well that money is not a substitute for love. Those of us who have been deprived of money may feel that money solves all problems. Money can help make a life more enjoyable, but human tenderness and affection can never be replaced by money. Mrs. Franklin Delano Roosevelt, frequently referred to as the First Lady of the World, often said that she knew well the worth of money, because she spent a lonely, unhappy childhood with a surplus of paper bills.

Money can also be used to express anger and resentment. The parent who is angry with a disobedient child may withhold money or an allowance. The parent who fears losing control over a young adult may attempt to maintain control through money. Money can symbolize dependence on and a sense of obligation to others. We can smolder with resentment at being in someone's debt. Money can be used out of fear, to placate a person, to bring him closer, or to get rid of him. It can also be used as an insult to a person, to pay him off, to keep him away. Some parents bribe their children with money or perhaps food to be "good," to be quiet, to be well-behaved, especially around guests, to help around the house. In this case, money can be used to replace discipline. Money can be used to express a host of attitudes and feelings in our daily family lives.

Newly married couples have to work out together how they can live with the money they have. Their previous attitudes and feelings about money come into play at the very beginning of their marital relations. Right from the beginning, married couples have to solve together their money problems. Although there are times when married couples do not have enough money for the necessities of life, and thus conflict, anger, guilt, fear arise, there are many instances when money becomes the focal point of arguments when the underlying trouble is of an emotional or sexual nature. In many marriages, a partner may use money as an excuse to pick a fight. Resentments of another nature may be expressed through money, as when a wife may get back at her husband through wild spending of money or a husband may show his anger at his wife by being tight with money. There are many variations on this theme.

Money means power and influence in our country. It can be used to gain power, maintain power, crush power, even in our own families. It is understandable that since money has such a powerful influence on our lives, we devote a great deal of time and energy in its pursuit. There are some of us to whom money is so important that it does not matter how we go about obtaining it. When money assumes power over us, morality and decency may go out the window.

The amount of money a person makes, the prestige level of his work, and the way he sells his personality are all important ingredients of success in our country. We tend to admire people more for what they own than for what they know or the kind of people they are. Frequently our conversations are loaded with references to money, and we rate people in terms of money:

> You look like a million dollars!
> He's not worth much.
> I'll bet my bottom dollar on her.
> Her price tag is high.
> She's an expensive item.
> I'll buy your idea.
> I'd give a thousand bucks for her popularity.
> He always has to add his two cents.
> He laughed all the way to the bank.
> His pockets are as empty as his mind.
> Think rich, act like a millionaire!
> He's good and loaded too.

She's a million-dollar item with priceless legs.
I wouldn't do it for all the money in the world.
I'll put my money on her.
Not for any money would I go with him.
I feel like a million bucks!

We are an affluent people. Our standard of living is high. The progress we have achieved in less than two hundred years is no less than stupendous. But progress is always made at a price. The countries in Asia are learning this. Until recently, the Asian family was the great source of security and stability. Each family, with all its close and distant relatives, was a community unto itself, responsible for itself and for the provision of its own means of protection and support. However, with the advent of industrialization, mobility, and the development of cities (urbanization), there has been economic progress in Asia. People who thought life could never be better are eating better, are freer of disease, are becoming literate, are living in better homes, are in closer communication with the rest of the world, and are having the pleasure of seeing their countries offer more opportunities to more people. But families are dispersing, young people are leaving the home earlier; the old, the sick, the handicapped, the retarded have to turn to the outside world for help. Small family groups are moving to the cities, where frequently there is no religious leader easily accessible, no family doctor to depend upon, no built-in sitters, no ready confidants, no reliable, experienced relatives around to turn to for help and guidance. Progress in the form of improved living conditions for more people is being made at the price of weakened family bonds. The concept of nationhood is developing; whereas before, allegiance was only to the family or the tribe. But the individual human being in Asia, as the individual human being in our country, is being put more on his own, is given more responsibilities, is more alone and lonely. Whereas the large family cared for the social problems before, today each person is more dependent on government, welfare programs, institutions, organizations, group endeavors. Decisions on marriage, employment, education, housing are more and more transferred from the dictates of tradition and ritual to the choice of an individual person.

As there is a constant shift from one set of rules and standards to another, the human being in the midst of rapid technological change is forced to rely more on himself. Freedom of choice puts heavy emotional burdens on us—we have to make decisions, and many of us feel afraid and powerless, as well as very much alone. Conformity to the dictates of "what other people think" is an attempt by many of us to relieve some of our emotional burdens temporarily. To be carried along by the wind and the tide can eliminate the necessity of our making choices and decisions.

Rapid industrialization, the rise of automation, high productivity, the increasing affluence of our people, the availability of consumer credit, mass education, the development of mass communication, advances in transportation, the powerful forces of advertising have all contributed to our high standard of living. The ever-growing number of products and services demands that we buy more than we need, strive for things we don't need or could do without, and possess things that everyone else has, whether we really want them or not. The advertisers have no doubt spurred the growth of our economy, but perhaps at the expense of our personal growth and maturity. They woo the public into buying more by telling us that we cannot live properly without their products, pitching at younger and younger groups to become buy-happy consumers.

The preschoolers who want to enjoy TV programs geared to them are bombarded with advertisements that train them to become an effective pressure group working on their parents to buy more. "Buy it for me now, Mommy, not later," demands the little one after watching several shows. Apparently this is what keeps our rate of prosperity going—demand, supply, more demand, more supply. In their book *Teen-age Tyranny,* Grace and Fred M. Hechinger devote a chapter to how the American business community has achieved its ambition to build up an enormous teen-age consumer market. The Hechingers show how business groups exert pressures on young people to conform to their friendship groups by using certain products and buying items they don't need. Those young people who are beginning to realize the impact of their purchasing power can use it to buy more selectively what they need and want and, conversely, can use the weapon of boycott when it serves their purpose.

In an attempt to seduce the public, and particularly young people, into more buying, advertisers today emphasize the speed and the magic of, and the minimum of effort required for, their products. They tell us that what is good is new, quick, unusual, easy, and certainly pleasurable. Unless these values are countered effectively in the home and in the school, many young people grow up thinking that anything that demands effort and that isn't new, quick, unusual, and pleasurable isn't worth doing. Any work worth doing requires sustained effort and often is accompanied by some discouragement and frustration.

Children do jobs at home because their parents ask them to and because their help is usually needed and appreciated.

All human beings like to feel needed, and children are no exception. Even a toddler likes to feel that he is involved in the swing of things in his family. Children like to receive a pat on the back, a hug, some praise for doing jobs and errands. Sometimes it is simply the fear of punishment if they disobey that ensures their cooperation; often it is the certain satisfaction that even the littlest youngster feels in doing a job along with others. Pleasure in accomplishment is deeply rooted in all of us. We feel pride when we are complimented by being asked to assume responsibility or to do a job.

Work is a basic part of almost every adult's life. It is an economic activity as well as a social activity whereby relationships are fostered, new friends are gained, and sometimes new enemies too. Working gives a person a feeling of being useful, of being involved in the swing of things, and sometimes of making a contribution to the world. The satisfactions and contentment we derive from work are important to our lives. When the head of the family is not content in his work, the whole family suffers. Naturally a man's work contributes to his feeling about himself. When a man is working at a job he enjoys, that interests him, that utilizes his potential and talents, what he does bolsters his good feelings about himself. What is dangerous is when his work becomes the sole determinant of how he feels about himself. So many people don't like their work and feel isolated and insignificant, and if they value themselves according to these feelings, they have a pretty grim picture of themselves.

If one is working only for monetary rewards, or if one has a certain kind of job because other people think that is what he should be doing rather than what he would like to do or is capable of doing, then the dull routine that accompanies such a job makes his work even more hateful. There is monotony in everyone's work. Even the President of the United States has some monotonous, repetitive, boring tasks and a certain amount of routine that is tiring. Routine gives us some structure and direction, and boredom of routine can be overcome by deep interest in our work. Also, we can live through dull routine and boredom when we receive praise and encouragement for our efforts. Some people can never keep a job because, they say, the routine is unbearable, the people are unbearable, there is a lack of opportunity. And they can always find more excuses. They find it impossible to keep any job for any length of time, even when they have skills that are needed. Why? Is it always the job, the people, the routine, or when this happens frequently to the same person, could the answer lie within him rather than outside?

In every employee's relationship to his employer, there are varying degrees of feelings that relate to the original child-parent relationship. Usually these feelings comprise both the tender and the hostile feelings one has toward his father or his mother. Some men cannot work satisfactorily with or for women. Some women cannot work well with other women or cannot work with or for men. Why? What were their feelings toward their fathers, mothers, sisters, brothers? How do these same people react to authority in general? Bottled up feelings of anger, carefully stored on some inner shelf, refuse to disappear and are sometimes the reasons for industrial accidents and errors, inefficiency on the job, violation of factory or office rules. Bottled up anger can cause sickness and absenteeism and, ultimately, unhappiness expressed in the inability to hold a job.

If you feel that you don't count at home, it may add up to your feeling that you don't count in school, that you don't count at work, and you may outwardly conform to all regulations while seething inside with resentment. Childhood feelings of never having been appreciated, can carry over to relationships with employers in later life.

Every one of us needs to feel we count, that what we do is appreciated, needed, useful. We need to be reassured that someone cares about us and recognizes the efforts we are making. The monetary rewards are important for many of us, but for many of us, love and approval count more than any wages earned beyond a certain minimum. When we care more for the salary than for the job that is to be done and still want approval from our colleagues and employers, we are asking for a great deal.

We attach enormous importance to a man's work in our country. Our work, as well as money, significantly affects our lives and our relationships. To many of us, the quality of our living depends on the money we earn and the work we do. If achievement, work, money are so important, can you understand how most men forced to retire at age sixty-five feel when they must stop working? What can replace the role that work played in their lives? How can they still feel useful? Many retired people feel that they have been retired from life and are no longer useful and needed. Some older people develop new interests and involve themselves in new work, but many go into depressions, get sick, and perhaps die sooner than they would have if they had still felt useful. You may laugh at the thought of preparing yourself for old age when you are in the prime of youth, but that is when the preparation is made. How can you prepare now for the day when you may be forced to retire?

What does it feel like to be unemployed in a country where work is so important? Some men will tell you that unemployment is a virtual emasculation, that it threatens their feeling of masculinity and lowers their self-esteem. Is it possible to feel useful and significant when not working? What are your attitudes toward work and toward future employment?

Today, close to a million out-of-school young people under twenty years of age have literally no employment opportunities. How do they feel? Many of them have dropped out of school, tried to enter the labor field, feeling inadequate and defeated because of difficult home situations and unsatisfying performance at school. When they enter the employment market, where, due to automation, more skills are demanded, they lack these skills. Their feelings of defeat, their fears of inadequacy are reinforced unless they are among the lucky ones who find a job or receive some special training. Young people under twenty make up one-twelfth of the American labor force, yet one-fourth of the unemployed are young people. Teen-age unemployment may become one of the most explosive social problems our country will have to face in the next decade.

It is not just the economic need and the unsatisfactory home and school experiences that force young people into the labor force early; it is also the pressure "to make good" —and quickly! Many a young man of sixteen convinces himself that he is wasting his time at school, that he will be happier on the outside, and that he will "be somebody" when he makes money. He dreams of having a lot of money, a car, a TV, special clothes. He may want plenty of cigarettes, liquor, gadgets, and conveniences, and he is in a hurry for these adult symbols. He wants to conform to the dictates of public opinion by attempting to fit into the definition of a "successful" person. Too often he finds out that his dreams and reality are miles apart, and he is disillusioned. He fails miserably because he has not developed the skills necessary for good employment. What does he do? Can he face going back to school and admitting defeat? Remember, our ads convince us that there is much "fun" in life and that almost everything can be easy and quick. In adulthood, in work, in marriage, in raising children, fun is intermingled with varying amounts of effort, boredom, tension, exhaustion, just as freedom is accompanied by responsibility and many painful choices.

School is not all fun and easy; it never will be and probably shouldn't be. Learning requires effort, interest, drill, and repetition. With encouragement and sympathetic understanding, we can try to make great strides in learning. But too often the schools ask for conformity to a certain kind of thinking and performance, for spouting the answer the teacher wants to hear, for achieving a jetlike rapidity of response to questions. Most of the time, students are rated by test scores and standardized procedures. To be part of a scaled mass called students discourages our participation and encourages our leaving the so-called learning box.

School should be a place where we learn how to learn and how to keep learning all our lives. Our schools need to give us (and some of them do, and some of them fail miserably) a sense of our own worth, encouraging us in what we can individually do and what we might be able to do. Creative opportunities should accompany the necessary drill and routine. When classes are crammed full of students and teachers are overburdened, it is impossible to encourage creative thinking. Students need to explore a hundred different answers to a question or problem without fear of being ridiculed or laughed at. Less emphasis on being "right" and more emphasis on original thinking is what students need to develop their minds and test out ideas. Feeling free to ask their teachers the questions on their minds and feeling free to challenge accepted beliefs prepare students for a lifetime of thinking. We are fortunate to have some teachers who are open to new ideas and who do not want their students to guess what the teachers want them to say. These teachers—and we need more of them—do not impose their values on their students but attempt to guide their students to the development of their own values. *A fine teacher can raise the sights of many lives.* Adults frequently refer to the teacher or teachers who influenced the course of their lives and helped them find themselves. Teachers can enhance our enjoyment of life. Teachers can introduce us to wonders we never dreamed of, to new worlds of interest that we can explore. Teachers with a radiance for learning spread it warmly among us. The plaintive cry today for better, more qualified teachers can be understood in the light of the powerful influence that teachers have on our lives. Fine teachers can prepare us to learn the rest of our lives, to open our minds and utilize the equipment we have for the betterment of ourselves and of mankind.

Some teachers are concerned only with exacting conformity to a certain syllabus or a particular way of thinking. The teachers who feel that they must have a ready answer to every question are the teachers who are usually unsure of themselves. They are bothered by the highly creative and gifted students who ask provocative questions, challenge their ideas, express original thoughts. The students who do not conform to "average" standards are regarded as bothersome by these teachers because they disrupt the routine. These teachers are frequently bothered by any students who are out of the ordinary. For example, medical authorities have learned in recent years that a significant number of children with reading difficulties have suffered some

mild form of neurological disturbance that they may overcome when about ten years old. These children are often
intelligent and able to keep up with their classes, but generally they are inconsistent, messy, physically and emotionally clumsy, and likely to overconcentrate on details.
They often interrupt more, and their feelings are more
visible and less controlled than those of others. Because
not enough of this medical information has filtered into the
schools for teachers to recognize and deal constructively
with these difficulties, these children have often been the
scapegoats of the classroom. It has been usual for them
to have difficulties in school and in their relationships.
When the difficulties have been diagnosed and when the
children have been encouraged by family and teachers,
they have responded well at school.

The highly gifted child and the child with difficulties
have often received the same treatment, because neither
conforms to the average or the norm. As competition increases, those who don't or won't conform are left out of
the average learning situation. It is a tendency in our country to regard learning as a means to a practical end rather
than as a goal desirable in itself. If the goal were learning
more for the sake of knowing more, then perhaps more
attention would be paid to the nonconformists in our
schools.

We need the encouragement of our parents, teachers,
counselors to help us discover our areas of competence and
our limitations in order to make the best use of our abilities.
The person who does not know what she is good at doing
(and all of us are good at something) will never be sure
of who she is. Our awareness and pride in being good at
something becomes part of our sense of being ourselves.

Every one of us respects competence. Competence in

building something, in fixing something, in learning, in fig-
uring out something, in cooking, sewing, sports, in organizing activities, in leading something, in art, music, dancing,
singing, in making up things, in being witty—all of these
talents are respected by us. Feeling competent in certain
areas encourages our self-respect, self-reliance, self-confidence.

It would be to our advantage to put more emphasis on
working together on projects under adult supervision at
school instead of competing so much against one another.
When we work together, we learn how to work with others,
how to get along with others, to respect the competence
of others, and we learn more about ourselves. Usually we
learn as much if not more of the subject matter through
cooperative enterprises as through individual effort. With
pressures to conform to the image of "success," many
parents, teachers, and youth leaders encourage sameness.
They fear showing favorites and fear that encouragement
and praise may make us conceited or headstrong. Could it
be that their fears about our areas of competence lie deeply
embedded in their fears about their own areas of incompetence?

To feel we have something to offer others enables us to
have more of a sense of belonging. To belong, to feel accepted, is important to all of us, particularly at the time
when we are struggling against our parents' authority in
order to achieve independence from them. We are uncertain,
unsure, full of conflicts. Often we love and hate our parents
at the same time. We need them and don't want to need
them. We are frightened. We feel all alone and confused.
Often we are ashamed of how our parents walk, talk, eat,
laugh, act with our friends. At the same time, we are proud
of them.

Basically we are all alone ourselves throughout our lives, for no other person knows all about us, how we feel, think, did feel, did think, want to feel, want to think. No one else knows how we feel about the most vital moments in our lives. No one else knows how we ache with loneliness sometimes. No one else knows, but *we* know. With the feeling of aloneness, we can still feel very related to others; but loneliness estranges us from others, for it is isolation, a feeling of being cut off from others. Aloneness can be delightful when we have time to do just what we want in privacy. Loneliness is never delightful. We may feel lonely at home with our parents when we feel that they do not understand us. When we feel lonely and cut off at home, we turn more to friends and to adults outside our families whom we admire. We are subject to much faultfinding, humiliation, criticizing, forbidding from adults in our high-school and early-adult years. Our friends support us, provide the reinforcement and encouragement that we get so little of elsewhere. We feel needed by them. We need them.

The lonely person, feeling isolated, may interpret these feelings to mean boredom. He may really be so unhappy with himself and his life that he will seek relief and acceptance in a group even if it means he must conceal or deny his real feelings. Most of us in the process of growing up conform strictly to certain friendship groups that are our anchors for a while. We follow the leaders, conform to the fads, the latest dress styles, the slang, the music and dance crazes, the popular beliefs and prevailing moral standards. Eventually many of us come to feel a sense of our own individuality by having safely sailed with the group.

We go from
valuing our parents' opinion and their way of life

to

valuing our friends' opinions and their way of life

to

forming our own opinions and way of life

based on

all the examples we have observed before.

"Everybody is doing it—why can't I?" we say to our parents when we want to do something. We may have parents who say, "Everybody is doing it—why don't you?" when they want us to do something. When "everybody" is so important to our parents, it is even more difficult for us not to follow what everybody else is doing and wanting.

There are parents who want to make sure that their children are in style, so they will buy anything or let their children do almost anything that is the current mode. "Oh, my parents let me stay up as late as I please and never set a limit on when I am to come home," may be said by a girl to her friend in order to impress the friend. The friend may relay this to her parents as the gospel. Foolish is the parent who does not check on this boast but accepts it in order to ensure her daughter's acceptance in the group.

The fears of our parents of our not being accepted may be their own fears of not being accepted, their own uncertainties about themselves, which may force us into patterns of behavior that they may not believe in, which may increase their own uncertainties.

Helping children to stand well with their friends is indeed important, but not when it means sanctioning activities that are against a family's code of acceptable behavior or standards. It takes courage for a parent to say, "But our family doesn't do things that way. I won't allow this in our family. It is not the way we live our lives." You may resent this now, but you will admire it later. When you are a parent, you will see how difficult it is to go against the tide of public opinion, and yet it must be done at times. Perhaps parents have to be stinkers some of the time, otherwise we would not have much to rebel against. Sometimes our parents' opposition can prove useful to us when we don't really want to follow a group pressuring us to conform, for we can say, "My old-fashioned parents won't allow me to do it," which might get us out of it.

Are you aware of the patterns of behavior you conform to? Are you aware of which group or groups you follow now? Do you adopt certain forms of double-talk or conform to fads of dress, even if they are not becoming to you, because they are part of the cult of your group life? Do you believe that eventually you will be able to decide what looks good on you and buy that rather than the latest mode, which may be uncomfortable and not becoming? Early adulthood and the high-school years are years of experimentation with clothes, which is why young people are known to have a fetish about clothes. Each group tends to conform to its own particular fashion, often modeled after the heroes of the moment. We are very concerned with our appearance during these years of learning about clothes and make-up. The fads of hair styles are also expressive of the attention we begin to give our appearance. Wild forms of hairdos, bleaching and dyeing of hair by both boys and girls sweep the countryside. The advertisers take advantage of our interests in appearance and style, provoke us into buying new items, trying new styles that often demand high hairdressing fees. Then they change the styles, and we change the styles. Sometimes we try to emulate the adult world, and other times we attempt to defy the adult world with our styles and our poses.

Do you smoke to look sophisticated with your gang of friends? Or is it simply that this is a way to rebel? Most of us try smoking in secret, and even through smoke-sputtered coughs we feel a secret delight through assuming an adult pose. Some of us grow to like it, or force ourselves to like it, and indulge in heavy smoking, particularly boys who want to fit the image of being tough or girls who want to look sophisticated. Many adults have not been frightened away from smoking by the medical world's strong warnings on the possible relationship between cancer and smoking, so many young people keep on puffing. Excessive smoking may affect only your own health, but excessive drinking can harm innocent bystanders.

Do you drink liquor? Do you enjoy it? Do you know why you drink liquor? Perhaps you take an occasional drink to seem adult or because you don't want to be considered a baby among your friends. If you drink a lot, perhaps you feel it takes you away from yourself and you can drown your sorrows in alcohol. Television and movies are full of adults drinking, and the social life of many adults centers around cocktails, so it is not surprising that young people want to drink also. If you model yourself after a toughy, naturally you want to consume some slugs as he does. If you model yourself after a movie actress, you might want to create the effect she does with a cigarette hanging out of her mouth and a glass of whisky balanced delicately in her hand. But people who are unhappy often seek comfort in liquor and try to escape from reality and their problems through excessive drinking. Young people (as well as older people) who are beset with uncomfortable feelings and problems may drink excessively, reducing the power of their consciences and lessening personal control, which in turn can lead to organized party-crashing, brawls of all sorts, unwanted pregnancies, destruction of property, injury, and even death.

Drinking and reckless driving are intimately connected. Yet many people drink excessively to be accepted by their peers and then endanger their own lives and the lives of others by driving. A car is a model of prosperity in our country. It is tagged with status for its owner. Many people in minority groups are denied opportunities for good housing and fair employment, but they can buy cars. The car, for them, is an outward sign of equality and is tagged with even more meaning as a status symbol. A car gives us freedom of movement and is often an instrument of independence. It can be a vehicle of escape, of zooming away from it all. In the early days of America, a horse and carriage could be used in the same way, but it was not as convenient for dating. Today a car serves as a recreation hall, a front parlor, a bedroom, a clubroom.

What does a car mean to you? When you are driving, do you glory in the power of being at the wheel? Are you sometimes awed by the responsibility that accompanies the power? A car can be steered to fit your wishes and can be geared to your aggressive intent. You can accelerate it so that you can go faster than those whom you think feel that they are better than you. You can race it against those whom you feel get in your way. Many accidents are caused by stored-up anger that is released when the person gets behind the steering wheel of a car. Some people assert themselves with a car the way others assert themselves with a gun. Police have stopped a number of young people exceeding speed limits who had a gun on the seat beside them —double-barreled power!

Speed seems so important to so many of us that we incorporate the urge to be ahead of others into our driving.

Speed-racing of cars, boats, bicycles, motocycles, surf-boards, even pets such as turtles, has become a fad. Flying, owning an airplane are becoming new uses of speed. Over the centuries, speed has been used as a measure of defiance and rebellion. Other indications of rebellion have been drinking, smoking, dotting speech with obscenities, using narcotics, stealing, fighting. When groups of us indulge in these activities, we are protected by one another in rebelling against the adult world while copying it to some extent.

Indulging in promiscuous sexual relations is required for membership in some groups of young people. Some experiment with sexual relations, risking pregnancy and venereal disease, only to gain acceptance by a group of people they like. Others who have no interests to pursue and feel isolated will indulge in sex with anyone who shows the mildest interest in them. Rebellion against strict moral codes at home, wishing secretly to punish parents or guardians, or craving affection and acceptance in a group lies at the root of many pregnancies among unmarried people.

When we feel unsure of ourselves, girls often seek the solidarity and backing of friendship cliques, while boys may join like-minded cliques or gangs. Some girls will join a group that is associated with a gang of boys. Gangs are not something new, although the newspapers and magazines often write about them as a new phenomenon. There are more people today and more city dwellers, more families and more broken family units, and thus more gangs. Today we know more about gangs, and some of their activities are destructive, so it appears as though they are more destructive than ever before. Juvenile delinquency and the moral depravity of young people today are being highlighted also. Twenty years ago, people were complaining of the terrible antics of youth, and many of the complaints were the same. The differences can be attributed to a greater number of young people today, more large cities and crowded living conditions, more cars, easier access to narcotics, more affluence among young people, and, probably, changes in adult behavior. Could it be that the destructive behavior we read about today is merely a different, more intensive form of the social problems of the past? Gangs have taken on different forms, but they have existed for many years here, and they exist in many other countries, because they offer something to young people that they don't find elsewhere.

A gang can offer a sense of belonging, of acceptance, a certain glamor, and strong loyalty bonds to young people. Close bonds of loyalty may not be achieved in school or in the playgrounds, and young people need the security of loyalty and close relationship with their peers. Poor facilities, the number of poor teachers, the pressures of stiff competition, a lack of understanding in the family can limit the opportunities for getting to know each other and learning to respect individual competences. Gangs make it possible for some boys to be full participants in something for the first time in their lives. For some, it is the first time that they are listened to and considered valuable. This may be the appeal that gangs can offer young people who cannot find these needs satisfied anywhere else. Gangs can replace individual conscience and can remove some of the burdens of responsibilities and decisions, which can make life simpler. Gangs are often the antisocial equivalents of adult groups and clubs.

Many adults live by group values. For many adults, quantity counts more than quality, and they belong to a number of groups. We are a nation of groups, clubs, organizations. Although adults don't wear Eisenhower jackets, tight pants, or have certain haircuts or hair dyes symbolic of membership, adults do have caps, rings, emblems, disguises, cards, handclasps to symbolize their belonging. The Elks, the Masons, the Rotary Clubs, and numerous others are based on the old formula of fraternization, fellowship, and general philanthropy. So are many women's clubs.

A number of new clubs have a specific aim and are centered on one aspect of belongingness. There are Alcoholics Anonymous, Divorcees Anonymous, Parents Without Partners, Suicides Anonymous (also known as Rescue, Inc.), Fatties Anonymous, Narcotics Anonymous, and on to the Vegetarian Brotherhood of America. Adults have gone so far as to develop clubs for The Little People of America, all under 4'8", and the Stratoliners Club, for those taller than 6'2", and the Bald Head Club, whose emblem is a bald eagle. Others are Mensa, a club for so-called geniuses with I.Q.'s over 150, a Procrastinators Club of America, The Liars Club, various "sneezer" clubs for victims of asthma and hay fever, an American Guppy Association, an American Fire Buff Association, and even the Chili Appreciation Society. There are adult clubs devoted to the love of cars, sports, animals, space themes, foods, wines, and on and on ad infinitum.

Would we have so many clubs if people did not feel so alone, so afraid and isolated? When family units were larger, more extensive, and more the centers of most activities, perhaps people were less alone and isolated and there was less need for outside groups. There is no doubt that the clubs and groups in our country were created to fulfill our needs, that they serve a purpose in our lives. Many of the groups offer opportunities for talking with others, sometimes communicating on a deeper level. Sharing sorrows, trying to work out common approaches to common problems, mass action on important issues have been the useful functions some groups have served. Others have served only to rein-force conformity and loneliness. Would we have such strict conformity to groups in high school if we did not feel frightened, unsure, and isolated?

Do we tend to feel small in the big, complicated world around us? The bigness of everything—from the bigness of our parents and other adults when we were younger to the bigness of buildings, cities, schools, government, labor unions, business, supermarkets—tends to encourage feeling small and powerless. The bigness of things, as well as the importance of "feeling big, acting big, spending big," has become a passion of our times. We have not only large eggs now, but extra-large jumbo size, and what's cooking next? We have immense shopping centers, vast merchandise-crammed drugstores, giant-size containers of soap, food, aspirin, and other household items, as well as "family-size" packaging of breads, cereals, and other foods. Many small businesses have merged into large concerns to survive. Many of us merge into groups to survive, because we feel that one person cannot speak out effectively, that only groups can.

Our lives have become small not only because of the bigness surrounding us, the overvaluing of material goods, and the emphasis on groups, but also because of the trend over the last twenty years toward using abbreviations instead of words, numbers instead of names, because we are trying to simplify our lives and save time, even though these procedures may not accomplish these aims. Telephone exchanges used to be names, which had more meaning to most of us than the present standardized country-wide tele-phoning procedure that requires us to dial an endless series of numbers. We have number names as identification, social security numbers, credit cards, punch cards, bank-account numbers, zip-code numbers, team numbers, group numbers, all kinds of code numbers—even sometimes at a reception or a party. Letters get addressed to "Occupant, 3232 44th Street"; it doesn't much matter who lives there. Invitations sometimes arrive saying "R.S.V.P. only if you cannot come," so what matters is how many will come, not who will come. All of this may be symbolic of economic progress, the pressures of time, and convenience, but is it not also symbolic of the mechanizing and automating of human life? Does the human being count as much as each human being should count?

Why is it that Americans are so clever at fashioning standardized products, standardized clothing, shoes, foods, autos, furniture, electric appliances, and so on? What is it besides our desire and ability to create higher standards of living for ourselves that indirectly standardizes so much of our lives? Have the very machines, conveniences, and systems that we have created to simplify our lives made our lives more complex? There is an apocryphal story circulating around about a wealthy widowed Victorian lady who lived in a Park Avenue penthouse and who finally decided to become very modern. She bought a dishwasher, a freezer, a washing machine, a dryer, automatic cleaning appliances, an automatic garbage-disposal unit, and a hundred other electrical gadgets. She promptly fired her retinue of servants and hired a full-time electrician—and then married him out of loneliness! Perhaps a certain amount of human contact and intimacy among family members, neighbors, and other people who come in and out of the house becomes unplugged when our machines get plugged in. The automated restaurants may be fine at late hours or when you are in a hurry, but they don't offer that smile, that human contact that some lonely people thrive on. Has conformity to the dictates of public opinion resulted in our hurry to get ahead, our substituting machines for people?

Perhaps the strong pressures to conform to the dictates of public opinion in our country have something to do with the fact that we are a mixture of many nationalities and racial and ethnic groups; we have had to, and continue to have to, create rules, traditions, and a way of life for all of us. Our so-called "melting pot" has united diversity under a red, white, and blue flag. We have thrived on diversity, and yet we strive for conformity.

Some of us want to eliminate differences or to ignore them, but this is difficult unless we eliminate some people or ignore them. There are differences, and these need to be expressed in any healthy society, just as in any healthy family. The people who want to avoid dealing with ideas they don't like, who want to ignore people whose principles they dislike or detest, often are the people who want to re-model everyone else in their own image and want to re-model the world into one neat package. The same people are likely to want to eliminate institutions such as the United Nations. For what is the United Nations but a gathering of the diverse? It is a forum for sharply diverging countries that may never share the same philosophies and conform to the same rules and standards that we do. The diverse are gathered together under a United Nations flag, with the task of trying to keep us all alive, free from war, disaster, deprivation. Our only hope is to listen to, to talk with, to deal with those with whom we disagree, in order to work out a consensus of action that can preserve the peace. Yet there are many of us who will not dare to listen to the convictions of those with whom we disagree.

Do you have any strong convictions? Are you willing to speak out when you disagree with others? Are you willing to commit yourself to an idea or a way of acting when you know that you might alienate yourself from people you like or admire? Are you willing to listen to others who disagree with you and face to face express your disagreements, then try to work out a plan of action if it is needed?

Is there anything you believe in strongly enough to fight for? Many people are afraid of expressing what they believe, because many people don't know what they believe, don't dare to believe in anything, don't respect themselves, or depend on the approval of others for their own self-respect.

If we begin to understand how little conviction we really do have, then we can develop convictions. When we plunge down through the many layers of beliefs that we think we have, that we think we should have, and that the people we like and admire have, we may begin to evaluate what is meaningful in our lives, what is important to us.

The great of all times dared to stand alone and be counted, dared to be less than popular, dared to be different, and we are grateful to them. Can *we* dare a bit more?

8. Love

WITHOUT LOVE, it is difficult to live. Without love, there can be no brotherhood of man, no group living, no civilization. All of us are born with a capacity for love. All over the world, people are nourished by love, encouraged to grow and develop by love. *Love* is an all-embracing word covering an immense variety of feelings, relationships, actions. It is through feeling love that we realize that we are not isolated from others, but together, interdependent. Being loved by and loving others are at the very heart of our lives.

We cannot measure, rate, or put love on any graph and compare it. It is something we feel in the depths within ourselves. Nobody can describe love accurately, because each of us experiences it differently and expresses it differently. Love takes on different forms and intensities with different people and under differing circumstances. There is a love we have for our families, for friends of the same and of the opposite sex, and for all humanity. When we are able to love, our love is expressed in the very way we live with ourselves and others.

We talk about being "madly" in love (are we mad?). We sigh as we announce we have "fallen" in love (from what height to what depth?). We shout that we are "desperately" in love (why so desperate?). Our mass media often support any confusions we may have about the meaning of love. Frequently it falsifies our image of love relationships, emphasizing the sexual aspects, the external qualities and behavior of people. We become wrapped up in a one-sided image of love that pictures love as physical attraction, infatuation, passion between male and female. When many of us speak of love, we imagine the romantic couples "in love" who snuggle in our advertisements, plays, songs, screen portrayals. We beam as we think of the loved one being showered with gifts, all kinds of niceties, and attention. Often, we long for "love" to come to us all neatly packaged.

But even if we romanticize love in this fashion, the way we talk about love in our daily conversations is not so one-sided. In our descriptions of people, in our questions, our evaluations of others, we employ the word *love* like this:

I would love to go out with you.
I love it just that way.
She loves the way the dress looks on you.
We all loved the grace with which she handled that.
She would love something to eat.
I would love to see that.
Do you love school?
I love the way our teacher treats us.
What he loves, he does well.
That gift meant a lot, so I loved it even more.
She couldn't have done it without your love.
It was a gesture of love.
That was a token of love for her mother.
She was loving with that child.

Our mass media frequently falsifies our image of love relationships.

She loves him enough to understand why he did it.
His love sustained her through thick and thin.
He loves his father too much to let him down.
You could see that each detail was a labor of love.
You could only ask that of a person you love.
Those were genuine words of love.

What does all this say? Look closely and see if you can substitute any of the following in place of the word *love: like, enjoy, admire, adore, respect, want, appreciate, to be interested in, to be fond of, support, trust, consideration, belief in, affection for, devotion, loyalty, kindness, gentleness, sensitivity, tenderness, understanding, effort, to be honest, to care for, to be responsible for, to feel free with, truth.* And are not these words a definition of love? Do we not spend our whole lives learning to develop our capacities to love other people?

At the beginning of this book, we were circling around the subject of love when we explored our early relationships with our parents. We were talking about love when we delved into the development of our feelings. When we probed feelings of fear, we found that they were often interrelated with our need for love. We could see that anger is love thwarted and that guilt is closely related to love. Rivalry and competition are often used as attempts to gain love. Strivings for popularity and conformity are expressions of the need for love. To like, to enjoy, to consider, to respect, to appreciate, to support, to trust, to believe in, to understand, to be honest with, to feel responsible for, and to care for others are what we learn in our relationships.

With love, we grow; with growth, we learn to love. When we have an unreal picture of love imprinted in our minds, we sit in waiting for Prince Charming or Cinderella to spring magically into our lives and, in a flash, sweep us off our feet, transform us, and solve all our problems. When this does not happen, we are unhappy. There are many charm courses, books, magazine articles that are quick to tell us how to make this happen, if only we would pay more attention to some prescribed magic formula. Usually, we are not completely sold on this because we know more than we think we do about love.

We have been dealing with love from the time we were infants. An infant's love is centered on himself, wanting his needs satisfied. It is his self-preservation. Love is felt and develops as an infant responds to and seeks response from others. Our mothers and then our fathers are the first people we love, if they were the ones to care for us and take care of us. Our love for them was a dependent love based on our helplessness and need for them. We felt, or did not feel, their love, which was our first textbook in learning to love. These initial lessons have far more influence on our relationships, our abilities to love, our ways of loving others and responding to the love of others than any book or any course of instruction on how to love.

We tended at some stage in our love relationship with our parents to be jealous of their love for each other. We wanted them to love us exclusively. We were not yet ready to care for others. With brothers and sisters, our family course of love was expanded and perhaps deepened. But brothers and sisters were also threats to the exclusive love that we may have wanted when we were younger. Grandparents, uncles, aunts, and cousins, as part of our larger family groups, sometimes provided special attachments, keen pleasures, new experiences, and new relationships that were part of our learning to love. Moments of anguish, of annoyance with demands put upon us, frequent frustrations, and tears accompanied family love. Love in families, as in all relationships, never runs a smooth, even course.

The close friends of our parents who were interested in us extended family love into new dimensions for us. They and the children who were our first friends and the parents of these children usually gave us faith in people outside our family nests. Most of us came to realize that there was love in the outside world, that we could be safe with others besides our own family. Our teachers in the early years could also assure us that the world outside the home was safe and could be loving. With more pages of experience, we learned that love could be expressed in different ways and could be more restrained than at home, yet meaningful.

We became aware of a new facet of love in our first few years at school when we established close friendships. Most of us trusted our friends enough to confide in them, to gripe with them, and often we tried to be like one another. We were testing out a new kind of love with contemporaries who were, like us, struggling to grow up. As the years developed, so our friendships developed, and with them, hopefully, a confirmation that the qualities of love could be felt in many corners of our lives. We learned that the content of love was such that not only pleasures and deep satisfactions, but bumps and bruises, burns and irritations were to be experienced. All of us at times experienced a certain turbulence in our relationships, as well as opposing pulls.

As children, we frequently indulged in hero worship and had crushes on older children and people who were contemporaries of our parents. Even if they ignored us, we created opportunities to see them and to model ourselves after them. These people, whom we admired—and loved, in a way—so intensively often represented a different way of life than what we had known. They introduced us to their ways of living, thinking, and doing things.

All the people we encountered in the early years of our lives instructed us in one way or another in matters concerning love. The people with whom we shared, confided, played, and worked, the people whom we cared for and trusted, those who tasted of our affection and we of theirs affected our growth and development. Our capacities to love were sometimes adversely affected by unhappy experiences that made us feel unloved. How we establish and maintain relationships with others are expressions of the development of our love and affect the relationships of our tomorrows.

We don't suddenly learn to love differently when we are dating or when we marry. Love cannot be isolated into one segment of our lives that has a ring around it. The kind of boy friend or girl friend we pick, or the kind of marriage partner we choose, is related to all our earlier loves. Many of us are surprised and can become angry when we learn that the people we marry are often versions, in one way or another, of our parents. When we reflect on our first, most intimate relationships, usually with our parents, it is not so fantastic that they are intimately linked with our marriages, which, under the best of circumstances, are our other most intimate love relationships. The resentments, the stored-up anger, and the conflicts that were unresolved in our child-parent relationships move on with us into our marital relationships.

If we have difficulty in relating to people generally, if we cannot establish and maintain friendships, it is to be expected that some difficulties will crop up in establishing and maintaining love relationships with persons of the opposite sex. If we grow up without parents, or with only one parent, and do not have an adequate substitute, is it not to be expected that we might have difficulties in our relationships with others, particularly of the opposite sex? The accumulation of our love experience enters into each new relationship.

Are you aware of any similarity or striking difference in the way in which you relate to family members at home and in the way in which you relate to others in the outside world? Has it been difficult for you to develop close relationships with people of the same sex? What about the opposite sex? Are your expectations for others (and for yourself) so high that no one seems good enough for you? Do you tend to feel you are not good enough for anyone else? Do you expect passion more than compassion to be the essential ingredient in any love relationship? Does that frighten you?

What we may interpret as love may not be it. What doesn't seem to be love to us may be it. It all depends on the picture we frame in our minds of what love is and how it is to be expressed. Love calls for expression. Feelings are expressed by gestures, body movements, words, and actions. Every human act expresses feeling as well as concerns, beliefs, and attitudes. We pat someone on the back to let him know we are with him, supporting him. We put our arms around someone's shoulders to bolster courage. We squeeze a hand, caress a head, hug and kiss to protect when there is fear or to affirm a friendship. Physical touch to most of us is often more reassuring than words, for it bespeaks a human tenderness.

Love, in its deepest sense, spells a oneness between two separate, unique human beings. Love is experiencing the differences, the uniqueness of each of us and thriving on these precious individual qualities. Together in diversity, we love. Sameness is not a requirement of love. With love, there is communication of minds, of concerns, of values and convictions, and sometimes physical communication.

There is a physical element in the expression of love that starts with a mother's fondling of her infant. In our families, we learn to express affection and fondness by the very way we are fondled. The love in some families is not demonstrative but is deeply founded on tenderness and concern. In other families, outward demonstrations of love are tenderly felt. When the familial base is sturdy with love, then our preparation for love relationships of all varieties is well begun.

As we grow and develop, it is apparent to most of us that love does not center solely on ourselves but flows into a concern for others. The good of others or of some others gradually becomes as important to us as our own good. This is part of the unity of love. It is growing from "I" to "we." From the local scene to the national scene to the international scene, there is a growing (sometimes painfully slow) concern developing by us for all of us. As we become closer to others, we become closer to ourselves and more capable of loving others.

The more we love, the more we can love; the more we understand about love, the greater our capacity to love.

Some of us have the illusion that we can love only once or that we can be loved by and love only a few people. We tend to talk at times as though there is a scarcity of love, demanding that love be rationed carefully. In our family relationships, as in dating relationships, we often worry about whether there is enough love left for us. But love feeds on love and expands and deepens and matures as we love, and there is no fixed quantity.

Respect and a genuine liking and enjoyment of one another are necessities in a love relationship. If there is no mutual concern, no respect and warm fondness, no sensitive understanding of the needs of each other, sexual relations between man and woman can become merely a form of private gymnastics. Sex as a force independent of love can indicate many things—vanity and hunger, resentment, revolt, and need for power.

The person who is not at all concerned for others, who is focused only on his own satisfactions, is likely to engage in sexual relations for his own gratification. We all want to feel pleasure in intimacy, but that does not mean it is necessary to disregard our partner. In all our relationships, it takes time for us to learn how to please another person as well as ourselves, but it helps if we are oriented to discovering the needs of others. When a person genuinely loves another and is concerned for his partner's gratification, these attitudes and feelings are expressed in his actions, including his sexual actions. We reveal ourselves in all we do. We carry over into our sexual relationships, as in all our relationships, the very strengths, limitations, and unresolved problems that make us the very personalities we are.

The sex urge is universal. With puberty, it is common for us to become more aware of having sexual urges and drives. We are more conscious of our bodies, for they are changing in shape and form and are more expressive of our coming adulthood. We are curious to know what sex is all about, what love has to do with it, how it affects us, and how it has affected the relationships of our parents and others we know. We ponder on this a great deal, discuss it some with our friends, and daydream about it, because it is important to us. Our curiosity about sex, our fantasies, what we do about it, with whom, to what extent, and how we feel about it all are different for each of us. But we all have the urges. Sometimes, we are not aware that these are of a sexual nature or do not want to be aware. Sexual urges can be stimulated by a touch, a sight, a thought, a smell, a sound, a taste, an act. We respond to tenderness, which may increase our desire. Our brain receives the message and, through our nervous system, sends reactions throughout our bodies. Our pulse rate may quicken, blood pressure and temperature may rise, muscles may begin to tense, certain glands may increase secretion, and our breathing may be affected. Desire can have a powerful effect on us even when we don't want it to.

We control desire in various ways. Some of us are ashamed of it, afraid of it, and control desire by denying it. If we do not recognize it, do not accept it to a certain extent, and do not channel it in various ways, we may eventually be controlled by unleashed desire. Some of us race to satisfy desire in every way we can, without regard for the people or situations involved, for we cannot control it. Most of us control our desires, our sexual urges, and do not deny them or let them trample over us. Instead we hold them in check for the appropriate person and appropriate time. Love builds its own controls out of the strength inherent in our concern for one another.

Dating is a trial-and-error period. It offers us the opportunity to see what kind of people we like and how we can like and love people in different ways. It acquaints us with how we ourselves deal with our desires. It can afford us the chance to see sex in perspective. We can appreciate the important role sex relations fulfill in our lives, but in proportion to love. Dating is more than physical contact for most of us. It is a way we come to know and learn to get along with people of the opposite sex and, specifically, to know and get along with one person. It is a valuable preparation for marriage in this respect.

There are some of us who do not allow ourselves the chance to date more than a few people, but, instead, tie ourselves up early with one person. Why? Perhaps we have had a stroke of luck and have immediately found the kind of person we had always hoped to find, and we wish to look no further. Perhaps we are afraid that we may not be liked by others and want the security of always having a date, so we go steady. There is a risk we take, there are uncertainties, upsetting moments, and bitter disappointments when we never know in advance whether we will have a date, whether we will be able to attend a party or a dance. Going steady can relieve these worries and pressures. But by going steady early in our dating experiences, we limit our opportunities for knowing different kinds of people, for expanding and perhaps deepening our experiences. Many a couple who went steady at fourteen and married at eighteen or twenty may feel cheated later in life and may then cheat on each other. Occasionally, childhood sweethearts continue to grow, individually and as a couple, and enjoy a basically happy and loving married life.

There are many forms of going steady. To some of us, it means a series of short, intensive relationships. Usually "going steady" refers to couples who go together over a long period of time, eliminating all other dating relationships. Going steady does provide opportunities to come to know each other well, to become part of each other's family life, and for parents to feel more at ease, perhaps, because they know the steady date. But the amount of time a couple going steady spends together, plus the intensity and concentration of the relationship, can make it difficult for them to apply the brakes in sexual relations. Occasionally the girl gets pregnant, and the couple is forced into a marriage or some other solution for which they are not or do not feel prepared. Of course, this can also happen even when a couple has not been going steady.

Any physical stimulation between male and female can lead to the next step, which can lead to heavy petting, which can lead to intercourse. It demands great fortitude and inner strength to know when to stop and how. Control is difficult, but the responsible couple who sincerely care for each other can apply the brakes. How far an unmarried couple will enter into sexual relations has not just to do with desire and attraction. It also has something to do with the individual needs of each partner, the communication existing between them, and the trust and respect they share for each other. Those who crave affection sometimes attempt to substitute sex for love and indulge in promiscuity. Some girls are not aware of how provocative their behavior is and how it arouses their dates. When there is communication between boy and girl on a date, problems such as these can be discussed freely, and boys will not be confused about what they take to be a "come on." Frequently, couples have the false notion that it spoils romance to talk about it. After all, in the movies they just don't sit and talk with each other about physical relationships. They fall into each other's arms and let nature take its course. Screen romance can be like that. But real life requires us to take down the screen and do our own thinking, feeling, and talking.

Many girls are persuaded that if they are free in petting, they can win and hold dates. They trade their bodies for popularity, but the trade isn't even, for this rarely brings them the kind of popularity that they seek. Instead, they are used by boys intent on gratifying themselves physically and then are scorned by the same boys for having been such an easy mark. Many boys will try to see how far they can go with any girl. They are testing. But most boys will respect a girl's wishes when she is firm. Some are not willing to control impulses or postpone satisfactions, because they are not really interested in the girl or cannot look beyond their own needs. This can indicate to a girl that she herself is not important to the boy. Girls more than boys tend to want some permanence in a relationship and to want thoughtfulness and consideration.

Some girls are seductive and actively seek sexual relations, but cannot admit this to themselves; they therefore put the blame and responsibility for control on the boys. Sometimes, they like to believe that they have been attacked or overwhelmed in a struggle when this has not been the case. Both boys and girls frequently tease each other with sex. The girl who leads her date on, excites him, and then stops abruptly and laughs is showing her need to place men in a ridiculous position in order to humiliate them. What man in her experience humiliated her? Could this be related to an unsatisfactory relationship with her father or some other family member early in her life? Our teasing with sex may relate to our fears about the power the other sex may have over us, which may relate to our fears about the power our parents had over us.

Intensive need for sexual relations can, at times, be motivated by our fears. Every boy, as every man, is at some time in his life anxious about whether he is sufficiently virile, masculine enough to be an adequate lover. There are times when every girl, every woman, is anxious about whether she is attractive enough to men or able to respond adequately to love. We all have these fears. It takes a long time, sometimes until after we are married, for us to realize that all women have some qualities considered to be masculine, even though they are predominately feminine, and that all men have some qualities considered to be feminine, even though they are predominately masculine. That this is true is not surprising, since ordinarily we are raised by both our parents, with their own qualities of femininity and masculinity, and we naturally tend to absorb some of these qualities. Then each country creates an image of what is considered masculine and what is considered feminine. Our worries about being feminine enough or masculine enough to fit the prevailing image in our country are part of the struggle of growing up. As we reinforce our knowledge of ourselves and become more accepting of ourselves and of our many imperfections of body, mind, and spirit, we are more competent to deal with these fears.

We all pick up misinformation, half-truths, and "dirty" stories early in our lives that can play on our ignorance of sex. If we divide love and sex and separate them from each other in our minds, then the stories we hear may encourage an image of sexual olympics for which we may feel we are woefully ill-prepared. We may conclude that we need some training and practice. A girl may fear that intercourse will rip and maim her vagina, yet may feel that she must experiment so that she will not be clumsy when she finds the man she loves. There are some girls whose fears and ignorance are such that they are convinced that kissing, with bodies closely touching, may make them pregnant, and so they may avoid all physical contact. A boy may fear that intercourse will harm his penis. He may fear that the vagina is a trap that can imprison him. This may reflect the fears he has about women. He may become superaggressive sexually, which is evidence of his anger against or fear of women. A boy or a girl may use sex as a weapon to get even with someone else, not necessarily the sexual partner involved. A boy or a girl may feel that practicing and experimenting will enhance skills in loving.

The training and practice we need is not in the form of techniques, positions, appropriate athletic actions at appropriate olympic moments, but it is in learning to care for and about others. In learning to love others, we learn to consider and respect the needs of others, to postpone immediate satisfactions, to take pleasure in pleasing others. We learn how vital it is to listen to and hear each other. When there is genuine love between man and woman, solidarity based on respect for differences, and intimate sharing of experiences, then sexual relations develop and grow with the love. Man and woman learn together what is best for them, what brings each and both the deepest satisfaction. Sexual ignorance and inexperience do not matter when two people share a concern, a tenderness for each other and a sensitivity to the invisible elements that flow back and forth in their relationships. Each experience is different and not necessarily appropriate for another, so we delude ourselves if we feel that we must accumulate experience in sexual relations. There are no set rules for sexual compatibility. It is not like learning arithmetic or spelling. We grow into love individually and as a couple. Our sex relations follow this growth. A marriage has its strongest foundations on friendship, although sex relations are important and indicative of the friendship.

What is a friend? Do you have a best friend? What is it about this person that makes her or him your best friend? What is it, in general, that you enjoy about your close friends? Surely you admire each other, respect each other, feel free to confide in each other. But what else? The genuine bases of friendship are trust and the freedom to be yourself without apology, without need for disguise. The real you is good enough for your friend and is, in fact, respected by your friend. You trust each other not to hurt each other knowingly. You trust each other to understand admissions of failure, to discuss personal difficulties. You will share ideas with each other, disagree with each other, and get plenty mad at each other when advice is unheeded. You are far more critical of a friend and quick to be irritated and annoyed by someone with whom you are deeply involved than with someone who does not matter to you. You matter to each other. You like your friend for the person he is, so you can disapprove of something he does without necessarily chucking the friendship. If you genuinely like and respect your friend, you can let him do as he sees fit and respect his right to think and feel and act as he does, and it is reciprocal. You can communicate your disagreements. You know each other's weak points and try to help each other overcome them. You can mutually help and give and receive without measuring it all into an account in terms of debts paid and deposits to be banked. With close friendship, responsibility is assumed when you feel your friend is in need. You don't wait to be asked, but you tactfully let him or her know that you are there to be called upon for help, and your friend does the same.

When friendship is of this nature, we do not have the time or energy to maintain more than a few very close relationships. Some people collect friends the way others collect stamps, coins, and matchbook covers. But such "friends" cannot be more than companions, for deep friendship involves love and a depth of giving and also of receiving. Some of us collect acquaintances but have no deep relationships, and others remain alone and prevent others from coming close to us. Some of us feel all alone and friendless. Why?

It is important for us to be able to establish and maintain friendships with people of the same sex. Some of us are able to do that but are fearful of establishing friendships with people of the opposite sex even when there is no sexual attraction involved. Could one of the reasons be that we may feel uncomfortable about the tenderness that is associated with any close friendship?

It is difficult for many boys, and many men, to show tenderness. We live in a country that plays up the tall, stoic, tough, rough, ultramanly aggressive man. Thus, many men feel they must conform to this image and are dissuaded from showing gentleness and sweetness. They will inhibit a tender gesture, frustrate an artistic bent, hold back on doing anything that might possibly be regarded as feminine, because they fear that their showing tender feelings will be scorned as weak or unmanly. Sometimes, the seemingly tough, pugnacious male may be disguising his feelings of inadequacy about being male by conforming strictly to the public image of aggressive manhood. The less tough-seeming man often has stronger inner fibers and more certainty about himself.

The boy or man who feels comfortable with himself and therefore is not threatened by the generally accepted masculine image of a man is more able to express tender emotion in public. Astronaut John Glenn could cry when he saw his wife Annie after his orbital flight. It was emotion that sprung from the depths within him that went into his embrace of his wife and his tears. He let go tears of worry, anxiety, tension, exhaustion, and perhaps of fear that he might not have returned. His moving emotion seemed to be a tender affirmation of his love for his wife and family. Wouldn't it be nice if he inspired more boys and men to feel that it is O.K. to be gentle and soft at times? Even in our relationships with our parents, many of us become self-conscious about genuine displays of affection, and, often, boys feel that they must never embrace or hug a parent. There are fathers who are embarrased to kiss their sons in public, or even in private, who would feel disgraced to embrace someone dear to them of the same sex who is in trouble or whom they have not seen in a long time.

Some women fear emotion too. Some women want to revolt against the stereotype of women as an emotional creature, and they purposely hold back on the expression of their feelings. There are women who are besieged with fears about not being feminine enough, and they may cover this up with poses and attitudes that they think they should have, that fit the generally accepted image of a truly feminine nature. Others try to prove their femininity through promiscuity or through enticing and teasing men. There are women who reject femininity so completely that they protest at being "treated like women," and some of them compete with men through work and achievement or in their families for power. The feminine woman can be in the home, in the office, can be anywhere in any guise, for there are many ways in which femininity can reveal itself.

Fears about not being masculine enough or feminine enough are related to fears of inadequacy in relating to others and in the capacity to love another.

Friendships, dating, going steady, and being "pinned" or engaged are part of learning to develop love for others as well as for ourselves. They are all relationships forming part of our preparation for marriage, which is only part of our preparation for embracing and loving mankind. Today, unlike yesterday, most marriages are decided by the two persons involved. Families have a lesser say than ever before. We are more on our own, more in charge of ourselves, responsible for ourselves, leaning on the weight of our own choices and decisions. The responsibility of it all, and the aloneness and sometimes loneliness, can hurry us into marriage for protective security. With the over-valuing of material objects, the bigness of an uncertain world, the mobility and rapid change occurring constantly, our feelings of inadequacy can overwhelm us and drive us into partnerships for which we are not really suited. We crave for a nest to come home to, where we can feel warm and snug and loved for ourselves. By expecting marriage to be a nest in paradise in which we shall be able to solve all our problems, we are being unrealistic and are likely to be disillusioned and to feel trapped and betrayed. For marriage means walking on solid ground. It demands a march of patience, perserverance, strength, concern, and understanding.

To some of us, marriage is only a legitimizing of sexual relations, and unless a love relationship develops there is no solid ground in the marriage. For others, marriage represents possession of another person, someone all for oneself —a return to the teddy-bear relationship of childhood. Some of us seek only protection or financial security. To others, marriage is the chance at last to be boss or to mold a person into the kind of person we want him or her to be. A marriage built on strong tender love and friendship does not lead to a struggle for power and domination, because each partner wants for the other what he or she wants for himself or herself. Each wants to guard the precious qualities of uniqueness. The courage and vision to see our loved ones in the true light of their frailties, imperfections, and irritating habits allow us to accept them for the people they are as we gradually learn to accept ourselves.

Acceptance allows communication; it allows us to listen to each other, to show a willingness to be present and hear each other out. To love out of strength, to give more than to need, is the triumph of a marriage.

We carry our bundles of unsolved problems with us to the altar. They don't and they won't suddenly disappear. The ability to see ourselves and our partners as we really are, not as a composite of the fears, the misunderstandings, the projections from our yesterdays, is our great and difficult task. To recognize the child within us, through deepening our understanding of ourselves, allows us to reinforce the adult within us. Reinforcing the adult within us permits us to be more in control of our feelings, more capable of a mature, tender love. No marriage has a simple melody, for there are bound to be some cacophonous, discordant notes and difficult chords along with the beautiful harmony.

9. Learning to Live with Ourselves

I T IS OUT of relations that we come to be. From these relations evolve our relationships, which, in turn, influence the unique personalities we develop.

The way we live our lives, the way we view our lives, our family life, the way we view our family life, the kind of persons we are, the kind of persons we think we are, and the kind of persons we aspire to be influence greatly the kind of people and parents we will be.

The greatest single factor in the breakdown of a person's mental health can be traced back to some failure or inadequacy in his relationships to others. Personality problems, job problems, school problems, sex problems, marriage problems, and a whole host of other problems can be related to problems in relationships. Some problems are related to economic conditions, to social conditions, to political conditions, to health, but more often than not, the core of the individual's distress lies in his relationships with others, and with himself.

All of us have problems, *not just you*, as you sometimes believe. The awareness you have of your problems and how you deal with them and live with them are the essentials. It is the degree to which these problems interfere with your well-being, the proportions they assume in your life, and the perspective in which you see them that determine the severity of the problems. Like almost everything else in life, our aim is to attain a certain equilibrium. We shall always have one problem or another.

The world is imperfect. We constantly strive to change it, to improve it, to better ourselves and the conditions of one and all. Our own country needs to rectify continuously the conditions that give rise to poverty, unemployment, poor housing, inadequate educational facilities, prejudice, discrimination, and physical and mental ill health among our citizens. As our knowledge grows with the testing out of new ideas, we develop new techniques and methods to combat some of these problems. Then new problems appear that need our attention. The ongoing struggle continues and sometimes frightens or overwhelms us.

Human beings are born to live with problems, with difficulties to surmount, or we would not be endowed with all the marvelous inner equipment with which to reason, to imagine, to reflect, to understand, and to love. Life is so precious to most of us that we tenaciously hold on to it. There are upheavals, explosions, battles going on in various parts of the world, and dangers that threaten us. Nevertheless, world-wide conditions of life for many people are better than ever before, and there are greater opportunities than ever before to help those in need. We tend, at times, to see only the disasters and the negative aspects of life. We view the world not only from a historical sense but by the light of our own experiences and attitudes. Do you tend to feel that the world is going to pot on those days when you feel that you personally are going to pot?

We can permit ourselves to be a little less tough on ourselves when we come to accept the imperfections of ourselves and others, the limitations of ourselves and others. There is not one among us who has not felt dissatisfied with himself at times. This can be an incentive to do something about it or can lead us into a depression or up and down various avenues of action. We all have had times when we have not felt adequate or capable or when we have been annoyed with our own social clumsiness. In reality, we are all blind at times, deaf at other times, certainly mute sometimes, often retarded in our ability to do what we want to do, and frequently maimed in some of our relationships. Rare is the person among us who has not suffered from some form of heartache. We are all afflicted with something. Some of us more so than others. We all have an "Achilles' heel," a vulnerable spot. Most of us find compensations for our physical and emotional handicaps in other areas of our living. There are some of us whose bruises heal, yet we remain scarred with bitterness throughout our lives. Those of us who have been encouraged to develop our competences are more aware of who we are, what we can do, and our roles in this world. We have less need to hurt ourselves when we are aware of our limitations and can respect ourselves and others. It then is more possible for us either to accept our imperfections or to put some effort into improving or changing ourselves.

Many of us suffer from expecting too much or too little of ourselves. Why? It may be because we have not yet achieved the self-respect that families, that schooling, that extracurricular activities, that friends and others who influence our lives can help us develop. The heart of our relationships is in the self-respect we do or do not feel.

Like almost everything else in life, our aim is to attain a certain equilibrium.

When we respect ourselves, utilize the tools of insight, tune in on our signals, our feelings, then our expectations for ourselves are not likely to be out of whack with what is possible to achieve. Sometimes we torture ourselves with the idea expressed by the word "should." We expect ourselves to do what we think we "should" do rather than what we are capable of doing. In the long run, nothing makes us more unhappy than having unrealistic expectations, for we can never attain these unrealistic goals or aspirations. It always ends up with our feeling defeated.

Our expectations for our parents are often impossible for our parents to live up to. We have been probing parents throughout this book, partly to deepen our understanding of their struggle with the most important and probably most difficult job on earth and partly to point up in what ways we prepare for parenthood by the way we have lived and continue to live our lives. When we accept the fact that parents are imperfect human beings whose development was greatly influenced by their parents, who are also imperfect human beings, and that all these imperfect human beings functioned in a family situation with the inner equipment that they possessed and developed, we are more likely to understand better our parents as they are today. Parents naturally make mistakes. Their shortcomings, their faults, their human frailties are keenly felt in family living. Parental responsibilities are not always pleasant ones, and their job demands that they be on duty all the time. It is inevitable that there are disagreements among parents and children, that each is often critical of the other. Most parents sincerely believe that they are doing what is best for their children. They probably are doing what they are able to do at this particular time in their lives.

Sometimes, with age, maturity, and experience, a parent

understands more, is capable of more wisdom, and can offer deep comfort and friendship to his children and to his grandchildren. Some devoted and helpful grandparents were not necessarily devoted and helpful parents. There are some cynics who say that the reason grandparents and grandchildren usually get on so well together is that they share a common enemy!

When we feel bothered by our parents, it is not only that they bother us but also that our dependence upon them bothers us. We tend to underestimate how difficult it is for us to launch ourselves in this world. Independence from parents is a life task for some of us; it is achieved earlier by others, depending on the quality of relationships in the home, opportunities for growth that were afforded, fostered, taken advantage of, or discovered by ourselves, as well as on what we were endowed with at birth.

The need to feel free, the need to be self-determined, is consistent with human nature. The struggle to be free is one of the outstanding features of history. Independence has always had to be fought for, but there are many ways to battle, and it need not be bloody. There is no one satisfactory definition of independence, because "surrender" to some people can be "independence" to others. It depends on the freedom to be what, to do what, to accomplish what? There is no particular predictable moment when you suddenly achieve independence from your parents and are launched into your own orbit. Human beings are not exactly known for their predictability. Independence comes slowly. The process is initiated when we take the first few steps forward on our own; sometimes we fall back and retreat, and sometimes we stand still before moving on again. You alone can feel—and probably will feel— your growing desire for and possible fear of independence.

With independence, your perspective changes and your relationships with your parents and others assume new dimensions.

The great Indian poet Rabindranath Tagore wrote some beautiful words about independence and freedom when he said:

Where the mind is without fear and the head is held high;
Where knowledge is free;
Where the world has not broken up into fragments by narrow domestic walls;
Where words come out from the depth of truth;
Where tireless striving stretches its arms towards perfection;
Where the clear stream of reason has not lost its way into the dreary desert sand of dead habit;
Where the mind is led forward by thee into ever-widening thought and action—
Into that heaven of freedom, my Father, let my country awake.

A democratic society like ours flourishes on the participation of its people, the decisions made and implemented by its people for its people. The will of the people in a democratic country is partly demonstrated by its choice of leaders, representatives, and spokesmen. The voluntary cooperation of groups and individuals to improve conditions of life and to help each other gives a democracy vitality and direction. All of us in America, whether we realize it or not, share a great responsibility. We have channels that we can employ to defend our beliefs. Even with our striving toward conformity, the individual human being in our country has some influence and can often act upon his beliefs. There are groups in existence that may represent our beliefs; we can join them if we feel that group action will be more effective than individual initiative.

It is, in one sense, easier to live under an authoritarian regime in which there is a prescribed way of behaving and thinking. There is one choice to be made: to obey the commands or to defy them and take the consequences. Channels of communication to express differences are not open in these countries.

In the newly developing countries, people who had allegiance only to families or tribes beforehand are suddenly learning the concept of nationhood. Many of them are slowly becoming aware of the responsibility of the individual in an independent nation. They are becoming conscious of their individual importance and their potential impact on their nation's policies. With the decline of colonialism and the upsurge of independence that has been achieved by so many countries in the last decade, more people are more on their own, more responsible for the lives they create for themselves. Young people go through the same process in relation to their own families that countries do in achieving independence.

With increasing independence from our parents, we inevitably struggle with increasing responsibility. We carry the weight of burdensome problems; we are faced with decision after decision that we must make, knowing that we are capable of making mistakes. When we search for our own identity, we are faced with new and different situations, and we must take risks. To live responsibly means assuming risks. We risk losing something in order to gain something else. We may risk our feeling of security when we place our trust in one person or follow a path that may lead nowhere. To have misjudged a person or to have missed a path that might have led us closer to our destination need not be a permanent defeat. We learn by our experiences. Hopefully, when we are aware of our mistakes, we learn from them, and they are wonderful teachers. We have to risk getting lost and wandering aimlessly at times in order to find out what we want for ourselves. The person who avoids trying something new, who avoids taking any risks, all too often is denied a passport to deep enrichment. Growth and development involve some experimentation and failure.

We need to try on new clothes to see how we look in them. We need to try new hair styles to see if they become us. We need to test out new activities to see if we like them. We need to think about and test new ideas, new ways of looking at life to find out what we believe, to develop convictions. Some of the new ideas will suit us, and some will have to be discarded. In life, as in cooking, when we know what our tastes are, we can experiment to see what we can add, subtract, change that will adjust a recipe to our tastes. Sometimes the results are delicious and rewarding. At other times they may be tasteless or disastrous. This is the risk we take. From what we learn by this experience, we can apply our knowledge to other recipes, eventually enabling us to devise recipes of our own. When constructing something, building something, fixing something, creating something, we are likely to experience the same process.

It is difficult for us to learn from the experience and advice of others, even when they are trying to be most helpful. In order for the advice to be meaningful, we have to want it and it has to be within the realm of our own experience. People do things differently; as a result, the advice we are given is often contradictory and confusing. Even in the simplest areas of living, we are forced to make decisions, to choose an approach, to select a method. Hopefully, we base our decisions on what is best for us and for those around us.

Certainly in a country like ours, where values are often contradictory, the decision-making process is even more difficult and demanding. The toughest part of a spaceman's job is making go-no-go decisions, which isn't very different from regular daily life. We learn early in our lives that what people do and what they say are often contradictory. In our own homes, we are aware of contradictions between professed principles and actions. Often we learn at home, at school, at work, ideas and values that not only differ but are opposing ones.

Historians indicate that starting way back in ancient times in Greece, conflicting and often contradictory values have dominated Western civilization. Sparta valued strict discipline, order, unquestioning obedience to the commands of the state. In Athens, the values of fulfillment for each human being, the free development of the mind, the enrichment of the person through creative and artistic opportunities were thought of as the only hope for the betterment of man. We in America have had our Spartan values, promoted by the Puritans, and have been greatly influenced by Athenian values at the same time. Success in terms of financial achievement may be an all-important value to some of us who give lip service to Christian ethics.

Are you aware of some of the contradictory directions that you are given? Perhaps the following examples of contradictory values will move you to create your own list:

Love thy neighbor.	BUT	Do unto others before they do unto you.
The kind of person you are counts most.	BUT	Success counts most.
Quality is to be achieved.	BUT	Quantity makes money.
The family is the core of life.	BUT	Business is the core of life.
Trust in God.	BUT	Never trust in anything.
Honesty is the best policy.	BUT	Get away with all you can.
This is a free country.	BUT	Public opinion dictates to us.
Be a rugged individualist.	BUT	Conform.
All men are created equal.	BUT	Some are born to serve, some to rule.
Patience is a virtue.	BUT	He who hesitates is lost.
New ideas are best.	BUT	Things should remain the same.
Hard work makes the man.	BUT	Do it the easy way.
It is never too late to learn.	BUT	Learning is for the young.
Education makes the man.	BUT	It's not what you know, it's who you know.
Crime doesn't pay.	BUT	Who's looking?

Contradictions and conflicts in the values of our country cannot simply be ignored or wished away by us. They are part and parcel of everyday confusion. Frequently we blame ourselves too much for our confusion and do not realize that it is a confusing world in which we live. Our task is to make sense of life for ourselves, and that means traveling with the baggage of confusion and doubt, making many stops along the way to rest and recover before going on.

As we approach adulthood, we are between two different worlds. We are neither child nor adult. At times, we choose to be ticketed as a child, while moving on tentatively and somewhat reluctantly to cross the border into the unknown world of adulthood. We want to feel needed and respected. Because we are deprived of responsibilities and opportunities we want, we feel frustrated and resentful. When offered certain responsibilities and opportunities, we tend to shy away from them and refuse them. We are torn between opposing pulls and experience many contradictions, particularly in our relationships with our parents:

Nobody understands me.	BUT	Don't try to understand me.
Don't give me directions.	BUT	Tell me what to do!
Why don't they love me?	BUT	They love me too much.
Why don't they spend more time with me?	BUT	Leave me alone.
Why don't they talk with me?	BUT	I won't listen to you.
Why don't they treat me more like an adult?	BUT	They expect too much of me.
Let me alone to be myself.	BUT	Who am I?

This is a natural part of growing up, although many of us tend to believe that we are the only ones torn between two worlds, feeling alienated and alone. Confusions, contradictions, conflicts are the bypaths we must explore to work out the directions we will pursue.

We are, in the years of approaching adulthood, like many countries in the world today where the high-powered Cadillac goes down a four-lane modern highway while the oxcart plods along the dirt path a couple miles away. The highly sophisticated modern businessman who travels widely and attends international conferences may still observe primitive rituals to ward away evils from his newborn baby or may consult with the witch doctors or fortunetellers when he is sick. To some degree, all of us incorporate the primitive and the modern within us. As with everything else, it is the degree to which this disturbs or inhibits us that makes it a problem for us.

Those of us who have strong religious beliefs are supported in our crises and can follow certain precepts that can guide us and help us. For those of us who are tourists in religion, never settling down to one set of beliefs, or for others of us who do not have religious convictions, the search for truths, for standards that we can live by is even more difficult. The search really never stops. When we become adults, we do not stop learning, or at least most of us don't. We can keep on learning all our lives, experimenting, changing, adding, and discarding, when our hearts and minds are open to exploration. This exploration must begin with ourselves. The truths we learn from a minor experience often apply to a major one. As our great philosophers have said over the years, there is no large or small in truth.

When we talk about an intuition we had that proved true or a feeling about something that proved correct, we are talking about the inner truths we have found in some experience of ours. Without being aware of it, we have applied these inner truths evolving from previous experience to another situation. This becomes a basis for judgment. Such judgment can usually be trusted, because it is based on signals from experience, depths of understanding within us. Often these depths of understanding are waiting for us to sound them.

The more we can decipher our own signals, the more deeply we know ourselves; the more we can govern our own actions, the more we can enjoy our lives.

"But I am confused by my feelings, and I cannot figure them out by myself," says many a person. What do we do in that case? Some of us struggle along and with great effort achieve a certain understanding of ourselves, along with feeling more in control of our lives. Others of us struggle alone and fall by the wayside or become servants to the dictators inside and outside us. Some of us make life miserable for ourselves and for others out of personal frustration. Others are pushed by outside forces into various conflicting directions. There are many people who want help and even recognize their need for wise counsel but don't dare to seek it out. Why? Is it because they fear that asking for help is a way to display to all the world their weaknesses and inadequacies? Perhaps the American tradition of self-sufficiency encourages this attitude among us. The immigrants with limited resources who on their own became great leaders stressed doing all you could for yourself by yourself, even though they themselves did not always do it all by themselves. It placed a stigma on those who asked for help, those who seemed dependent on others, and the stigma remains with us today.

The person who shows courage is not the person who shies away from asking for the help he needs. It is the person who seeks help when he needs it who demonstrates courage. His desire to develop himself as best he can, his acceptance of his need for reinforcement, insight, and support, and his feelings of responsibility in not letting others down are not signs of a weak person. When we are very dependent upon our elders, we do not listen to what they say, for we may fear showing them how much we depend upon them, we may fear the truths in what they say, and our anger, our guilt, and our fears obstruct communication.

The art of listening to others without necessarily accepting all that is said is an art worth developing. It enhances communication. But our feelings can prevent us from hearing, as they can prevent us from seeing, touching, tasting, smelling. The wonders of human beings and the beauties that exist around us are never appreciated by many human beings. The tender thrill of seeing a child grow and develop before your own eyes, the surprise and delight of seeing a plant flower or looking at an orange sunset, the joy of touching or being touched by a loved one and the wonder of different textures, the delicious tastes of superbly cooked food and the sweetness of freshly picked vegetables, the magnificent fragrance of a rose in bloom and the pure smell of a healthy baby's breath, the tingling sensation that travels throughout the body when the voice of someone we love is heard after a long separation, and the swelling pride and admiration we feel when we hear words of meaning and impact being orated with passion— these are profoundly moving experiences of everyday life that many of us have enjoyed deeply. But many of us are unable to enjoy these things. A new intimacy with life can begin and we can see more of the beauties around us when we are helped to become closer to ourselves through a better understanding of ourselves.

When we need help, sometimes we turn to our religious groups, to a teacher we admire, to a school counselor, to a relative we trust, and sometimes we need only confide in our good friends and family members and openly discuss our problems. Sometimes we need only a long, quiet conversation with ourselves. However, there are times when we must seek professional help. Psychologists and psychiatrists must charge high fees for their kind of work, and if we cannot pay these fees we may find a clinic where we can be helped. In the telephone book we can find social welfare agencies staffed by social workers who offer services to young people and/or to families. It takes guts to make a telephone call of this nature and to inquire where help can be found. But when a whole life of enjoying, loving, working productively is at stake, the discomforts of seeking help are relatively unimportant.

What kind of help? Different people require different kinds of help, and there is no pat solution that fits everyone. Social scientists have discovered that some people cannot be helped through the usual methods of individual counseling and therapy, but that the whole family must be treated. For those of us who never really had a family, who grew up without the tenderness and compassion that many families give their children, new ways of helping, new approaches must be and are being explored.

Seeking help is the first barrier, and then we move on to accepting the help we seek. The people who run aid programs and give technical assistance to countries are aware of how important it is for people to want aid, to accept it as a means of helping them to help themselves. Administrators in social welfare and relief work have frequently encountered the resistance, the resentment, the hatred felt by recipients of aid who don't want to change, who might want everything done for them, or who expect overnight solutions to their problems. It is the same for the individual human being who seeks emotional aid.

All of us need help in growing. Sometimes we need more help from others than at other times. Some of us require more assistance than others. Some of us profit more from aid than others. Exploration into ourselves demands that we connect our bodies and our minds to our feelings and our attitudes, for these are all intimately related and do not operate separately. Sometimes our doctors can help us when our bodies are signaling that our feelings are exploding. Our oft-forgotten childhood cannot be left to overshadow us but needs to be probed and incorporated into our adult lives. It is hard for some of us to do this probing alone.

Exploration means delving into unfamiliarities. Have you ever thought about the word *familiar* and how much of our security lies in that word? It suggests a family, belonging to a family, where everything and everyone are well known and where there is a recognized way of behaving. As we grow up, we learn certain cues that trigger behavior that become as automatic as our breathing. These cues are as important a part of our education as the spoken language, the values, and the beliefs our parents teach us. When the cornerstones of familiarity are weakened by unknown, untried, uncertain situations, it is normal for us to become upset and anxious.

Those of us who have lived abroad know well that we are often at sea without familiarities. Familiar ways of acting, familiar gestures, familiar tones of voice, familiar ways of thinking and organizing life—all these familiarities that we have depended upon without realizing it are suddenly missing when we live in a foreign country. We are stripped bare of a protective covering and must depend on our inner resources to build a new life incorporating part of the past and adapting to the present. The absence of familiarity can create even tighter, more intimate bonds within a family unit, or it can challenge a person enough to enable him to grow splendidly. Conversely, the absence of familiar surroundings can be the last straw in a poor marriage, or it can reveal a very unstable person who may have been hiding behind the façade of familiarity. Some preparation for the unfamiliarities in living abroad eases preliminary aches and pains.

Some preparation for the unfamiliarities and uncertainties of adulthood can also ease some of the aches and pains. The young adult is traveling along untried routes, meeting unforeseen difficulties, dealing with unfamiliar situations, and walking toward more uncertainty. When we were little children, the world tended to be full of certainties. We took them for granted. Some of us continue to treat certainties as human rights. But as our years on earth increase, our uncertainties multiply. We know more truths yet raise more questions, knowing that the full, complete answer can never be found by us. Our incomplete knowledge of God is perhaps symbolic of our incomplete knowledge of man, or perhaps our incomplete knowledge of man is symbolic of our incomplete knowledge of God.

We can be fine workers, fine doctors, fine craftsmen, fine lawyers, fine businessmen, fine engineers, fine writers, fine drivers, fine mechanics, fine artists, fine scientists and yet be so tyrannized by inner forces that our relationships are woefully inadequate. As skilled as we may be in other areas, if we are not skilled in establishing and maintaining relationships, our lives suffer and the lives of others may be adversely affected. World history is affected by the inner life of the human beings who make great decisions. Important decisions in almost any endeavor can be dictated by inner needs not really related to the matter in question. This is the reason we so desperately need more human beings in this world who cannot be tyrannized by forces within or outside themselves.

There is no substitute for a fine human being in this

world; there is no replacement for a person who keeps on questioning, examining, exploring himself. The world needs more reason and logic, more imagination and creative thinking, and the world can have these resources when more of us attain more self-knowledge, self-respect, self-confidence.

We are constantly changing, forever being faced with new problems demanding new solutions. The world is always in need of new ideas, new proposals, and constructive uses of old ideas and old methods. Change is one of the few constants in life. It is one of the few certainties we have. Every one of us changes. Not all of us continue to grow, to learn, to examine. Hopefully, most of us will keep on growing, learning, examining, illuminating our vision the rest of our lives. In order to better understand other orbits, we must better understand our own. We are aided in our inner explorations by knowing how to use the sharp tools of insight, becoming more aware of our own inner signals and being able to decipher them when necessary, and by constantly deepening and widening our horizons.

The conclusion to this book can be written by only one person—*you*—for the search will be carried on by only one person—*you*.

If you want a magic formula, it is on the next page.

INSTANT MATURITY!

WHY SETTLE FOR LESS?

> without fuss
> without thought
> without bother

in one easy step
proven 84½ times as effective as anything else . . .

YOU CAN SAVE TIME WITH brand-new
> different
> messless
> snap-cap
> flip-top
> pop-up
> built-in
> premixed
> ready-to-use Maturity.

IT TRANSFORMS YOU IMMEDIATELY.
A MIRACLE THAT IS THE REAL THING!

Everyone will love you!
All relationships A.O.K!

with

INSTANT MATURITY
DON'T YOU WANT IT RIGHT NOW?

> Sorry,
> there
> is
> no
> easy
> answer.

SOME QUESTIONS FOR
FURTHER PROBING

Who am I? Do I feel pretty good about myself despite occasional ups and downs?

What am I capable of? Have I had enough opportunities to find out?

Do I have any solid warm relationships?

Can I maintain friendships? Is there any friendship involved in my dating?

What words would I use to characterize "growing up"?

Why is parenthood one of the most important yet most difficult jobs on earth?

How have families changed since Grandmother's day?

What changes have I noticed in family living just in the last few years?

With industrialization, mobility, urbanization, what benefits have we received and what liabilities?

How do we learn techniques to work out conflicts? (Describe a conflict situation in which you were involved recently and how it was worked out.)

Why is it so important to learn early in life to make choices, to come to decisions?

Why is it vital for us to be in touch with our feelings and have opportunities to release pent-up feelings? What am I likely to do when I am angry? (Name the ways in which anger finds expression.)

How can anxiety and confusion help me? What can I learn from failures?

How has my self-confidence been bolstered lately—and by whom? Do I praise others when they deserve it?

Why don't Americans emphasize more the great reservoirs of past experience that make it possible to create the new? Why do we emphasize the newness of things and tend to believe that anything that is new is good?

Why do Americans ask young people to grow up fast and be sophisticated? Why do we tell our older people to stay young?

How have advertisements come to play such an important role in our lives?

Can we educate a mind and ignore a personality? Should we?

If it is only a family that can educate hearts, what happens when there is no family or a family that has fallen apart?

What are our schools educating for? What is the purpose of education? Who are the people we really are educating?

What is your definition of a responsible person? Can schools teach responsibility through civics?

How can we reach all the minds of all the people?

Does the American educational system cry out for new and perhaps revolutionary thinking?

Could a person with a sense of his own worth kill another human being? In what situation?

Can a healthy person become ill for emotional reasons? (Give an example.)

Who benefits from poverty?

Who benefits from discrimination and prejudice?

Who benefits from disease and ignorance?

What are some of the primitive superstitions that I cling to? What superstitions or myths did my parents believe that I have come to reject?

What strong convictions do I have?

What can I personally do to make this a healthier, more peaceful world?

What is progress?

BIBLIOGRAPHY

BARUCH, DOROTHY W.: *One Little Boy.* New York, Julian Press, 1952.

BINGER, CARL: *The Doctor's Job.* New York, Norton, 1945.

BRAMELD, THEODORE: *Ends and Means in Education: A Midcentury Appraisal.* New York, Harper, 1952.

DUVALL, EVELYN MILLIS: *Facts of Life and Love.* New York, Popular Library, 1956.

ERIKSON, ERIK: *Childhood and Society.* New York, Norton, 1950.

FRAIBERG, SELMA H.: *The Magic Years.* New York, Scribner, 1959.

FRANK, LAWRENCE K.: *Society As the Patient.* New Brunswick, N.J., Rutgers Univ. Press, 1950.

FRANK, MARY H., and LAWRENCE K. FRANK: *How to Be a Woman.* Indianapolis, Ind., Bobbs-Merrill, 1954.

FRIEDENBERG, EDGAR Z.: *The Vanishing Adolescent.* New York, Dell, 1959.

FROMM, ERICH: *Escape from Freedom.* New York, Holt, 1941.

———: *Man from Himself.* New York, Holt, 1947.

GINSBURG, SOL W.: *A Psychiatrist's Views on Social Issues,* New York, Columbia University Press, 1963.

HALL, EDWARD T.: *The Silent Language.* Garden City, N.Y., Doubleday, 1959.

HIRSH, SELMA G.: *The Fears Men Live By.* New York. Harper, 1955.

HORNEY, KAREN: *The Neurotic Personality of Our Time.* New York, Norton, 1937.

KLUCKHOHN, CLYDE: *Mirror for Man.* New York, Whittlesey, 1949.

LANE, HOWARD A. (Mary B. Lane, ed.): *On Educating Human Beings.* Chicago, Follett, 1964.

LYND, ROBERT: *Knowledge for What?* Princeton, N.J., Princeton Univ. Press, 1939.

MACKENZIE, CATHERINE: *Parent and Child.* New York, Sloane, 1949.

MAY, ROLLO: *The Meaning of Anxiety.* New York, Ronald, 1950.

MEAD, MARGARET: *And Keep Your Powder Dry.* New York, Morrow, 1942.

MONTAGU, ASHLEY: *Helping Children Develop Moral Values.* Chicago, Science Research Associates, 1953.

————: *On Being Human.* New York, Schuman, 1950.

NEILL, A. S.: *Summerhill: A Radical Approach to Child Rearing.* New York, Hart, 1960.

NORTHWAY, MARY L.: *What Is Popularity?* Chicago, Science Research Associates, 1955.

OVERSTREET, H. A.: *The Mature Mind.* New York, Norton, 1949.

RIDENOUR, NINA: *Mental Health in the United States.* Cambridge, Mass., Harvard Univ. Press, 1961.

RIESMAN, DAVID: *The Lonely Crowd.* New Haven, Conn., Yale Univ. Press, 1951.

SIEGEL, ERNEST: *Helping the Brain-Injured Child.* New York Association for Brain-Injured Children, 1962.

STEIN, M. R., *et al.* (eds.): *Identity and Anxiety.* New York, Free Press, 1960.

SUTTIE, IAN D.: *The Origins of Love and Hate.* New York, Julian Press, 1952.

WAGENKNECHT, EDWARD (ed.): *When I Was a Child,* an anthology. New York, Dutton, 1946.

WHITESIDE-TAYLOR, KATHERINE: *Do Adolescents Need Parents?* New York, Appleton-Century-Crofts, 1938.

FOR FURTHER EXPLORATION

BUTLER, SAMUEL:*The Way of All Flesh.* Harmondsworth, England, Penguin Books, 1950.

CANFIELD, DOROTHY: *The Deepening Stream.* New York, Harcourt, Brace & World, 1930.

EWALD, CARL: *My Little Boy.* New York, Scribner, 1906.

FRANK, ANNE: *The Diary of a Young Girl.* New York, Modern Library, 1952.

GIBRAN, KAHLIL: *The Prophet.* New York, Knopf, 1946.

GRIFFIN, JOHN HOWARD: *Black Like Me.* Boston, Houghton Mifflin, 1960.

HANSBERRY, LORRAINE: *A Raisin in The Sun.* New York, Random House, 1959.

HUGHES, RICHARD: *A High Wind in Jamaica.* New York, Modern Library, 1932.

LAWRENCE, D. H.: *Sons and Lovers.* New York, Viking, 1958.

MILLER, ARTHUR: *Death of a Salesman.* New York, Viking, 1949.

NUTTING, ANTHONY: *Lawrence of Arabia.* New York, Signet Books, 1961.

ST. EXUPERY, ANTOINE: *Wind, Sand, and Stars.* New York, Reynal & Hitchcock, 1939.

SALINGER, J. D.: *The Catcher in the Rye.* Boston, Little, Brown, 1951.

SCHULBERG, BUDD: *What Makes Sammy Run?* New York, Modern Library, 1952.

SMITH, BETTY: *A Tree Grows in Brooklyn.* New York, Harper, 1947.

SMITH, LILLIAN: *Killers of the Dream.* New York, W. W. Norton, 1961.

STEINBECK, JOHN: *Of Mice and Men.* New York, Viking, 1937.

WRIGHT, RICHARD: *Black Boy.* (In various paperbacks.)